Miracles Among Chaos

A Courageous Journey Through Childhood Abuse and Mental Illness

B E L L A   L O U I S E   A L L E N

Come with me as I walk through time and heal my own demons …

authorHOUSE®

AuthorHouse™
1663 Liberty Drive
Bloomington, IN 47403
www.authorhouse.com
Phone: 1 (800) 839-8640

Published by AuthorHouse 12/15/2015

ISBN: 978-1-5049-6757-0 (sc)
ISBN: 978-1-5049-6758-7 (hc)
ISBN: 978-1-5049-6756-3 (e)

Library of Congress Control Number: 2015920459

Print information available on the last page.

Any people depicted in stock imagery provided by Thinkstock are models, and such images are being used for illustrative purposes only. Certain stock imagery © Thinkstock.

This book is printed on acid-free paper.

CONTENTS

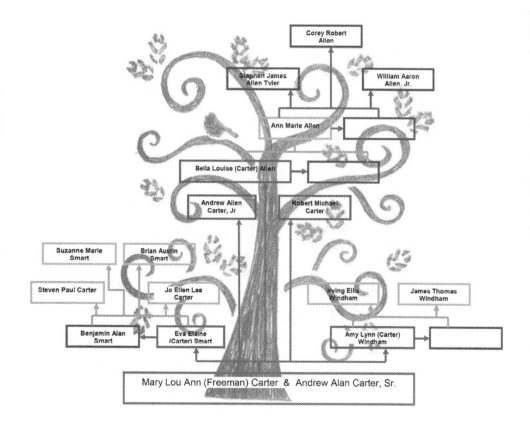

FAMILY TREE

Bella Louise Allen (Carter) - July 21, 1967

William Aaron Allen Sr. - December 5, 1964

Ann Marie Allen - January 31, 1990

William Aaron Allen Jr. - January 29, 1993

Corey Robert Allen - December 27, 1994

Mary Lou Ann Carter (Freeman) - January 8, 1943

Andrew Alan Carter Sr. - September 6, 1937

Eva Elaine Carter (Smart) - May 4, 1961

Steven Paul Carter - April 15, 1983

Jo Ellen Lea Carter - April 15, 1983

Suzanne Marie Smart - July 13, 2000

Brian Austin Smart - July 13, 2000

Amy Lynn Carter (Windham) - September 1, 1962

Irving Ellis Windham - December 23, 1987

James Thomas Windham - December 27, 1989

Andrew Allen Carter Jr. - January 30, 1964

Robert Michael Carter - June 24, 1966

DEAR READER

I am a mother, a daughter, a sister, and a woman not unlike many of you. I wish to share a journey, one of much abuse. My journey has been hard and long, and yet what I wish the most is to share the gifts that I have received throughout the years.

The greatest gift I can give to you in reading my story is the gift of forgiveness. In order for any of us to heal and to move on, we must forgive our perpetrator, our assailant, and yes, even our family. In reading my book, you will witness the abuse I suffered as a child through my father's own ignorance. You will see the denial that my mother went through to "save" herself from her own fears.

As I share with you my journey through life and struggle with the effects of my childhood abuse, you will learn of my mental illness. I am diagnosed with bipolar I with PTSD. I will show you a side of myself that I am not proud of. I know in my healing process, my journey here on earth is exactly what God has planned for me.

As I write my story, I remember the things that I have tried to forget for the past forty-seven years. I have learned things about myself that I never even knew. I first started writing my journey *Miracles among Chaos* back in 2006 when I had my first manic episode with my bipolar and was hospitalized.

I share with you in my writing the faith that it has taken me to get through just one day, one hour, and even one minute. My journey while here on earth and the wonderful people I have met and even the not so wonderful people have helped form the strong, loving, kind person that I believe myself to be. I have witnessed many miracles straight from the hand of God. I have witnessed too many tragedies to even make it into my story. I want the miracles that I have witnessed to touch your lives and your heart and remind you to keep the faith, for *Miracles among Chaos* is what we all share.

Bella Louise Allen

Introduction

The farther backward you can look, the farther forward you are likely to see. — from a fortune cookie

I learned early on the love for reading and writing. You can sit all day on a comfy couch or never leave your bed. You can enter into worlds afar and be lost to the wonders of the imagination.

This book has been painful in the making and enlightening as the pages unfold my own mystery of self-discovery. I first dreamed of writing my story in July 2006, but the actual first words were not put to paper until June 2014. I hope to help my children understand me a little better. I hope to erase the memory of fear and pain somehow with the words that I put to paper. I hope to help my children understand that, yes, I am a strange and unique woman. The journey that I traveled through childhood and young adulthood into motherhood helped form the woman I am today—all while battling ghosts from my childhood and a mental illness they call bipolar and finally being diagnosed with PTSD.

The struggles I have endured are just a glimpse of how much a mother truly loves her children. I hope someday you, the reader, can look back on your childhood and find some remembrance of a happy childhood. I believe if we all search hard enough, there are good times in our childhood that can somehow outweigh the bad. To each one of us, I dedicate this book to our inner child. I will share the good, the bad, and the ugly and heal myself through my own story. I hope you enjoy my life's journey, for it is how I became the woman I am today.

Bipolar, the Disease

Definition: bi-po-lar dis-or-der (N). A psychiatric disorder characterized by extreme mood swings, ranging between episodes of acute euphoria and severe depression.

Bipolar disorder, formerly known as manic depression, is a mental illness that brings severe high and low moods and changes in sleep patterns, energy levels, thinking process, and behavior.

People suffering from bipolar can have periods where they feel overly happy and energized and then periods where they feel sad, hopeless, and sluggish. They can feel normal in between these two stages. You can think of the highs and lows as two "poles" of mood, which is why it is called "bipolar" disorder.

PTSD—Post-Traumatic Stress Disorder

PTSD is a mental health condition that is triggered by a terrifying event, either by experiencing it or witnessing it. Symptoms may include flashbacks, nightmares, and severe anxiety, as well as uncontrollable thoughts about the event.

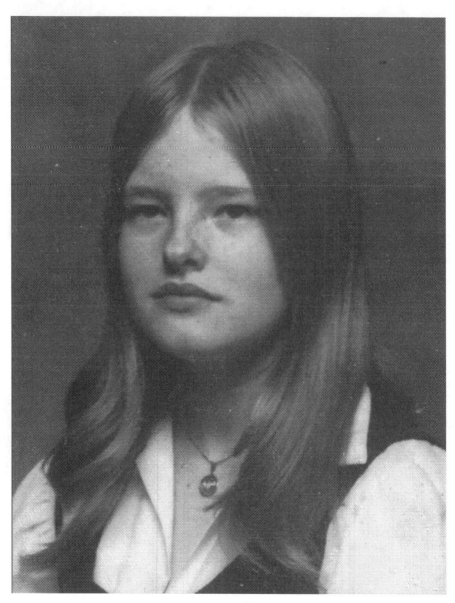

Amy Lynn Carter

CHAPTER 1

Shattered Dreams

My life living with bipolar disorder started around the time I was in high school. I was fifteen years old. I, of course, was not aware that I had the disorder until after my first diagnosis and hospitalization in July 2006. I was diagnosed with bipolar II.

My life was a constant up and down of emotions. At the time, I believed I was just your typically emotional fifteen-year-old girl with hormones running wild. I thought my childhood dramas were causing my swiftly moving mood swings.

I remember one day at the age of fifteen, it seemed like my life was crashing in on me. The day started out like any other day. I got up at six to beat the rush of four siblings to get to the bathroom and get ready before the bus came to pick us up for school. There usually was a squabble or two to get into the bathroom. I made the rush that morning and got on the bus at seven, arriving at school by eight. Things spiraled out of control from there. I don't remember much about that day other than that I had a major meltdown. In the corner of the hallway by Mr. Long's history class, I lost it. My loyal friend Olivia came to my rescue yet again that morning.

I cried uncontrollably to Olivia in the middle of the hallway that morning. I am still amazed to this day that not one teacher took notice of my emotional outburst. I just hope that today this kind of outcry for help would not go unnoticed. I believe the outburst that day had to do with the fact that my father was unable to refrain from going at night to my room and standing beside my bed to masturbate. At the time, it seemed to be a nightly routine. This happened for many years. I cannot pinpoint a start time for this behavior; I just remember it happening. My father would come to my bedroom almost nightly. I would lie awake, waiting, almost holding my breath for his footsteps. I listened for the squeaking of the floorboards. I would get as close to the wall as I could and pull the covers over my head.

I remember during the summer on hot, humid nights not being able to breathe. The blankets were up over my head so I wouldn't have to watch in horror as my father pleased himself. I was hoping he would not get close to the bed. The nights when the cat came into the room were the worst. My father would have an excuse to get close to the bed while he was naked. He would reposition the cat over and over on different spots on the bed.

My father would be naked in the bedroom with the lights on. He would fondle himself, masturbate, and move the cat around on the bed. I would stiffen. My whole body would be tense the whole time he was in the room doing his routine. I remember the sound of him masturbating, his breathing, his clearing his throat trying to control himself. It seemed to go on forever every night.

So yes, I believed my world was crashing in around me. I wanted the nightmare of reality to stop. How could I ask Olivia to help? I couldn't even help myself.

Shortly after my meltdown at school, my older sister Amy confronted my mother with the fact that our father had been doing exactly the same thing to her. If we had thought that hell did not exist, we all found out that night that it surely did.

I don't remember the exact confrontation. However, I remember things went to hell in a handbasket really quickly. There was a lot of whispering. Amy had taken my mother to one of the bedrooms to talk to her. When my mother came out of the bedroom, I had never seen her so mad in my life. Amy trailed out of the bedroom behind Mom. Amy was trying to explain, telling her that Dad had been doing it for years.

I remember my mother and my oldest sister, Eva, trying to piece together the information Amy had given her. They had all of the photo albums out on the table. They were trying to put a time frame on the accusations she had made. They frantically looked for clues that they knew they didn't want to find.

It took me awhile to figure out what was going on. My mother said, "I don't believe you. You're nothing but a little liar."

Dad was sleeping in his recliner in the living room. After he woke up he had figured out what they were talking about. Mom confronted him, and he was out of control. He was pacing back and forth like a caged animal. Dad started screaming, and then he started hitting Amy. His fists flew, hitting Amy over and over. She tried to get away, but she was never quite quick enough. I heard Amy pleading for him to stop. The screaming and hitting and pulling of hair seemed to go on forever. I saw hair flying— Amy's hair flying through the air. *Oh my God,* I thought. *Will he ever stop?* I thought for sure he would end up killing her. He was so out of control, so angry.

How do you help someone in a situation like this? I was scared to death. I was sitting in the fetal position with my knees up to my chin in the corner by the buffet. I closed my eyes. I tried to shut out the screaming that I heard. I covered my ears with my hands to muffle Amy's screams, her pleas for him to stop. I tried to block out the events that were unfolding before my eyes. I opened my eyes and stared. I focused on the brown wood of my mother's buffet that was right in front of me. I stared at it for what seemed like an eternity. Then I heard nothing—no screaming, no pleading, and no more beating her with his fists. I remember then coming out of my trance.

I was in total disbelief that my mother would not believe my sister. My mother believed my father over her own child. Why would a child make something like this up? My heart sank, and I knew this incident would change all of our lives forever.

My father was a brave man that night. How could he have known that I would not spill the beans? How could he have known that I wouldn't tell my mother that he was masturbating in my bedroom the same way he did with Amy?

My father went around in a panic, almost scared of what we might say. He was still out of breath from the beating he had given Amy. He pointed with his large, calloused finger and asked each of us in turn, "Have I ever touched you?"

He went down the line asking Eva, Andy, Robert, and then me. He asked us all the same question, and his eyes were wide with what I thought was so much anger. Looking back, I now think it may have been just a little bit of fear—fear of what I might say. As he came to me, I was still in the fetal position on the floor. My arms were wrapped tightly around my legs. I thought to myself, *This is the only way I can get him to stop his nightly routine of coming to my bedroom.* But I was so scared to get a beating like I had just witnessed Amy getting. The only thing that came out of my mouth was, "No, you have never touched me."

In a way I guess I didn't lie. He had never touched me, not that I can remember. My poor sister Amy, after being so brave and having the shit beaten out of her, didn't remain living with us very long after that. She ended up moving in with an elderly man about one week later. She ran errands and did housework for him. He only lived about a mile and a half down the road. Amy went to school in the next town over. She did graduate from high school, and I was so proud of her. She survived that night, walked out of our trailer, and found herself a place of shelter and continued her education. She didn't look back once. I was so lost without her, and yet I envied her strength.

She wouldn't know until many years later how she saved me from the nightmare of my reality. Shortly after Amy's confrontation, my father stopped his nightly visits to my bedroom to masturbate. Thank you, Amy, and thank you, Jesus.

Shattered Dreams

Dreams come to us in an unconscious mind.
Dreams come from our desires, hopes, and fears.
Green, beautiful meadows, with deer frolicking playfully,
White, fluffy clouds floating, flying, magical,
Life brings you back, back to reality.
Shattered dreams are all you have left,
A life filled with pain, loss, and disappointment.
My shattered dreams lie on the floor
Like shards of glass, sharp and unforgiving.
I am no more innocent to life's lessons.
I struggle to go on with my dreams, scattered to the wind.
As I try to collect the pieces of my shattered dreams, I feel the pain.
The pain is more than anyone should bear. Even with my shattered dreams, I
Forge on through to peace and love and forgiveness thanks to you.

Amy, Andy, Eva,- front Robert & Bella Louise

CHAPTER 2

Childhood Memories

I was born on July 21, 1967, and I was the fifth and last child my parents would have. I had two sisters. Eva was the oldest. She was born on May 4, 1961. Amy was born September 1, 1962. Andrew, whom we called Andy, who was named after Dad, was born January 30, 1964, and Robert was born June 24, 1966.

Mom didn't get much of a break in between the births of the children. With Eva being only six years older than I was, I can only imagine how overwhelmed my mother must have felt having five little ones so close together. Raising children back in the 1960s was so different than raising children today. The Department of Human Services didn't seem to exist or have watchful eyes on the children back then. Today you see abuse cases almost daily on the local news. It is horrifying to read the paper or watch TV.

Women had a different attitude toward marriage, self-image, and raising their children back then. It was almost your duty as a young woman back then to get married, have children, and be a dutiful wife. If there were complications of any kind in the marriage, you didn't share it or talk about it. Divorce was pretty much unheard-of. Disciplining your children was also very different. In our house it was "normal" to receive harsh punishment—mostly from my father—for any behavior that was not acceptable. The punishment could change like the wind changes in the leaves of the old oak tree. One day it was harsh and ferocious, and the next it was calm and gentle.

Eva, my oldest sister, was always Daddy's little girl. I don't remember her ever getting into trouble; I remember feeling that she could do no wrong. Eva, however, shared with me that that was not how it always was. She did tell me that her abuse was never like the abuse that the rest of us received. Eva told me of an incident where Dad had beaten her with a belt and left welts all over her body. Eva said she went to school and had to change for gym class. She remembers the other kids at school staring at her because the welts Dad had left were visible for all to see. It is amazing how five children can grow up in the same house and all have similar, yet different, memories. I thought all these years that she was somehow special and that daddy had loved her more than the rest of us. It's amazing how as children we block certain events out to protect ourselves.

Amy, the next to the oldest child, was named after my father's mother, Grammy Amy. In order to understand the relationship that Mom and Dad had with Amy, you would have to understand their relationship with my grandmother. It was as if all the hate and dislike they had toward Grammy Amy were channeled toward my sister Amy. My grandmother had red hair, and Amy had an auburn tone to her hair. Amy also had lots of freckles, just like Grammy. I remember the relationship between my grandmother Amy and Mom was always strained. Mom hated Grammy Amy because of the way she had treated Dad. This my mother told me. Mom also told all of us that she wasn't going to throw Dad away like his mother did.

It was like my mother could do no right in my grandmother's eyes. I felt my grandmother thought she was better than my mother and father. She definitely favored her other grandchildren over us. She always bragged about how well they were doing in school and all the things they had or the trips that they had been on. I remember spending time at my grandmother's house, and I had the honor of sitting through a piano lesson that my cousin Lisa Marie had. My grandmother paid for these lessons. None of us ever received anything from her aside from a game that we got one year—"Go to the Head of the Class." It was a board game. That's all I ever remember getting for Christmas from her, and we all had to share it. I know Christmas is not supposed to be about the gifts, but even at that young age, I knew how she felt about all of us. As a child, we could sense the hostility and distance on my dad's side of the family.

The relationship between my dad and his own mother could be a story all by itself. My grandmother Amy got pregnant out of wedlock, and this was back in 1937. I can only imagine the gossip and ridicule that went along with this pregnancy. I heard how Dad's Aunt Evelyn and my great grandmother Elsa Carter had to convince my grandmother not to give him up for adoption.

The story goes that my great grandmother and great grandfather and Aunt Evelyn raised my dad for the biggest part of his life. My dad would spend short periods of time with his mother, but the majority of the time he was with his grandmother and grandfather. So I think my father's feelings for Amy stemmed from his feelings of abandonment by his own mother. Andy, my oldest brother, was my father's namesake, and his relationship with my father was not a lot better than that of Dad and Amy. I believe Dad saw a lot of himself in Andy, and he didn't like what he saw. I believe he was harsher on Andy than he was on Eva, Robert, and myself.

I remember Robert being a quiet boy. He and I were pretty close, not just in age but as a brother and sister could be. Robert had some medical issues with his ears and couldn't hear well. I remember when he had his ears operated on, and I remember how sick and helpless he looked. For the most part he stayed out of Dad's radar of anger fits as much as he could. Not by any means did he receive the wrath of Dad on occasion like I did.

My memories of my childhood come in clips or slots of memories. I have some good ones, but more bad childhood memories. As I dig into my memories, I hope to pull more detailed and better memories from that lost place in my head and in my heart.

Just a Wee Lass

It was 1971 and I was four years old when we moved into the new trailer. My first memory of living in the new trailer was the place where I slept. I slept in the hallway in a white crib where most people put the washer and dryer. I remember the feeling of being exposed. Exposed and vulnerable to what I don't remember. I remember I would wet the bed nightly. I remember I would wake up being cold and wet. The smell of urine will never leave my memory.

My earliest memory of hating my dad, being disgusted and wanting to crawl away and hide in a hole somewhere deep in the woods, was when I was five years old. It was summertime, and I had spent the past two weeks at my Aunt Rosa and Uncle David's house. I remember the overwhelming feeling of being homesick. I missed my mom and probably my brothers and sisters.

I remember it was my birthday, and it was a happy time for me. Every child is supposed to have good memories of his or her birthday, right? There was a cake, and I was excited to get gifts. The only memory other than being excited is wearing a red dress. I had a pageboy haircut that my aunt had given me while I stayed there those two weeks. As we celebrated my birthday, being five should have been so great, but my memory is just a feeling of disgust, hurt, pain, and loss. My memory is of innocence lost on my fifth birthday.

My dad picked me up to hold me. I had my birthday card from him. I wanted to get down, but he held me tight. He read the card to me. He called me "Daddy's little girl." I got a slobber kiss on the cheek, and I felt sick to my stomach. I remember stiffening; I held my breath, and I didn't want to be his little girl. Not if it meant him doing "that."

I still do not remember him doing anything until I was like nine years old. How do you block out such a horrible thing?

Naked as a Jaybird

My next memory of hate, disgust, and total exposure to the world was when I was nine years old. I had small, developing breasts; I know I was young, but I developed young and started my menses young. I grew pubic hair young as well. It was a hot summer day, and it had been raining all day. I remember Andy and Robert and I were outside in the pouring rain, and we were already soaked to the skin. We ran around and jumped in those big awesome puddles. Being kids, we weren't thinking about the consequences of our actions.

When Mom and Dad came home, however innocent our actions were, the reaction we got was fierce. It was out of control and almost filled with hate—hate for each of us. There was screaming and running around and chaos. I remember scrambling to change my clothes. My mind was racing—*Oh, God, oh, God ... he's going to kill me.* When I was naked, just between getting my wet clothes off and trying to get my dry clothes on, Dad came into my bedroom. I remember covering myself as best I could. *Which do I cover first, my small budding breasts, or my crotch that was trying to get hair on it?* The only thing I had to hide myself with was my arms and hands. The embarrassment was unbelievable, and then came the fear. Always the fear—what would happen, how bad would it be this time?

Dad came in screaming, "What were you thinking, *huh*, *huh*? Ruining your shoes out in the mud puddles?" As he went on and on, he beat me with his belt. He loved to take that belt off and make us put our fingers in between the leather and *snap* it. Tight and hard. It hurt so much. My eyes closed tight every time the belt hit my soft white skin.

Daddy, Get Your Gun

I guess looking back I should feel lucky I wasn't one of my brothers or sisters. I remember the day Dad took after Andy. My brother had run away from home. For how long I do not remember. He was staying with the neighbors up the road—my first crush, Brian, and his family. Andy had been caught at the store stealing a package of bologna to eat, and he was arrested. The cops called my mom at work, and she had to bail him out of jail. All I remember is the screaming and rushing around, and then poor Andy took off down the road. All I saw was his back turned to me, and his legs were going as fast as they could. Dad grabbed a rifle and took the car, the little yellow Pinto. He went after my brother with a loaded rifle. My memory stops here. I assume Andy went into the woods. I have no idea what happened after he got home. This is just one of the worst memories I have of my father's rage.

As I remember these bits and pieces as I go along, I wonder to myself how a child can come out of such horrible abuse and not continue the horrifying cycle. I knew very young that I did not ever want to pass on this legacy, the abuse, the unimaginable terror that we lived with each day.

Just Plain Cruel

One day my dog Baxter would not lie down fast enough or in the right place, and my dad took after him. Dad grabbed a broom and started to hit him. Baxter may have been a Doberman pinscher, but he was the gentlest dog in the world. Baxter let my nephew, who was just a baby, walk on his scrotum, and Baxter did not bit him. That's how gentle my dog was. My full-grown Doberman would sit in my lap at the table to be close to me. When we went away, he would sit on the kitchen table and wait for our return. He slept under the covers of my bed at night, even during hot summer nights, just to be close to me.

When my dad had Baxter cornered in my room one night and was beating him with a broom, Baxter did the only thing he could. He growled and snarled at my dad. My dad threatened to kill him. Dad must have feared him or got over his fit because he left the room and Baxter was still alive.

I remember when I was probably twelve, and I had gotten a kitten from a friend of mine. Her name was Kitty. She had long black and white fur. Kitty wasn't very old, and she wasn't quite housebroken. When Dad found out that Kitty had an accident on the floor, it was all but the end of the world. My dad had the boys put my kitten into a brown paper bag, and they took her out back of our trailer. I'm not sure, but I assume it was my dad who put several rounds of his rifle into the brown paper bag and killed my kitten for having an accident on the floor. I don't remember crying, I don't remember feeling the panic and knowing what was going to happen, and I don't remember the shots that were fired to kill my tiny little Kitty. I just remember it happening.

My brother Robert had a cat named Jasper. My father took Robert to the dump to shoot his cat. Jasper was always getting into fights and had pussy sores on his face. Back in those days, we as children rarely went to the doctor, so Jasper would certainly not be going to the vet. Dad just gave Robert and Jasper a ride to the dump. Dad left Robert and his cat on the dump road after giving Robert the rifle to shoot his cat. Jasper didn't come back, so the job was done. To my dad's surprise, three weeks later Jasper came strolling into the yard. Dad of course thought he was seeing a ghost.

It scared the shit out of him. Dad was so pissed, he made Robert do it for real this time; Dad went to the dump with him and made sure it was done.

I remember having a beautiful German shepherd pup. Her name was Annabella. She was full of energy and had separation anxiety, which I don't believe was heard of back then. Annabella got bored one day while the whole family was out of the house. She literally ate a chair. She chewed the arms of the chair off and also ate the seat. It was a completely ruined chair when we got home. My mom was so mad, she hooked Annabella out on a lead outside for two weeks straight. She of course got fed and watered, but being hooked outside was not a pleasant thing for such an active dog. The day my mom decided to release her from her punishment, Annabella had gotten loose. When we got home from school that day, there was Annabella lying beside the mailbox dead, with her tongue hanging out and her eyes wide open. I do remember crying for the loss of our sweet little Annabella. Mom felt really bad, as did the rest of us.

After graduating from high school, I went to work in another state for a short period of time. Mom decided she wanted a puppy, and while I was gone away, she took my dog Baxter to the humane society and got herself a new puppy. I was mad and devastated to think she thought so little of him to just give him to the humane society. To this day I don't know if someone adopted him or if he was euthanized.

This is where I really felt upset, even though Annabella and Baxter were just dogs and Kitty and Jasper were just cats. To me it was like losing a family member. Death for a child in itself is a traumatizing event. So how does a child get over the cruel intentions and deliberate animal-like actions of killing or disposing of part of the young child's family?

Bella Louise Allen

The Animal Within

He is quiet and stealthy,
Lurking here and there.
Beware not to awaken
The animal within.

You cannot see him until it is too late.
You will not even know how you woke him.
Do not wake him from his slumbering sleep,
The animal within.

It may not be you he seeks this time.
It may be one of those you love.
You wonder, fear, wait somewhere near
For the animal within to maim, harm, and even kill
The gentle, kind, trusting you. Please beware!

Mom, Bella Louise, Eva, Amy, Dad, Andy & Robert

CHAPTER 3

Like Clips from a Black-and-White Movie

My Mother's Desperation

I will never forget the day the bank came to foreclose on the land. Mom and Dad had been struggling to pay bills, and I remember for years during the fall and winter Mom being laid off from work. Even though I have some good memories from this, it caused additional hardship for all of us. When Mom was laid off during the winter, it seemed good to see my mother. She would be home when we all arrived home from school. The house would be filled with the wonderful smells of a stew that Mom would throw together out of leftovers from the day before. I especially loved it when Mom would bake raised glazed donuts or applesauce oaties (a family favorite cookie) that we all devoured.

Things always seemed to be financially tight. We never had new school clothes, and if you were lucky, you would get hand-me-downs from somebody. This day I will never forget because my mother was screaming, crying, and pleading for them to not kick us off the land. The bank had come to foreclose on the land and take our home. My mother screamed, "I am not going to lose this place." Where would we go, five children and two adults? Somehow my mother convinced them not to kick us out that day. My Aunt Suzie lent my parents the money so we didn't lose our land or our trailer. Thanks be to God!

Emergency! Emergency! Don't Dial 911

The day we all went riding bikes down the Pember road was memorable. It wasn't too far up the road, but the ride into the Pember road was a rough one. It was winding and downhill. It was part dirt road, part grass road. It wasn't traveled very often, so it was pretty dangerous for riding bikes down. I was on the handlebars of my Cousin Donnie's bike, and as we were going down this hill, I tried with all my might to stay on the bike. I was wearing flip-flops and didn't notice the spokes to the bike were cutting into my big toe as we went flying down the hill. He steered left and then right all the way down. As Donnie went down this winding unsafe road, my foot flew into the spokes, coming out and then going in again. Over and over my foot hit the spokes of the bicycle tire.

I started screaming for Donnie to stop, and when he did, I had a huge gash in my big toe clean to the bone. It was a long and painful ride back to the main road and then to our house. How we got hold of my grandmother Amy, I don't know. Mom and Dad were working, and there was no way any of us would call them at work. So, Grandmother Amy came and got me and took me to the little hospital in town where we attended school. I had my toe wrapped up, got a tetanus shot, and off I went to go home.

My mother was so pissed. I don't remember a reaction from Dad, but Mom was pissed. We didn't have the kind of money to be going to the doctors for cuts and scrapes. It wasn't just the fact that we had been riding bikes where we shouldn't be. Someone got hurt and called my grandmother Amy of all people. Then we went to the hospital, which my parents could in no way pay for. Growing up, unless you were on death's door, you did not go to the doctor's. No questions asked.

Kids Being Kids

In our little town when you got bored, you found things to do. In the summer of 1975, I was eight years old, and my sisters were thirteen and fourteen. They both had "boyfriends," which I'm pretty sure our parents didn't know about. We were bored hanging out all day long, and it was hot. We went down to the swimming hole on Lover's Lane. It wasn't far down the road, and it sure would be nice to get cooled off. My sisters and I and Eric and Mike went down to Lovers Lane to go swimming. The boys decided it would be so much better to go skinny-dipping. I was mortified, being only eight years old. My sisters do not remember this, but I remember seeing butt cheeks that day. Being only eight years old, I was the worst tattletale ever. When we got home that day, I told Mom what had happened. She could not believe that they had taken me down to Lover's Lane and the boys went skinny-dipping.

The Club

We spent a lot of time with my friend Brian and his family. We played baseball games, made forts, and played hide-and-seek and all the other fun games that kids would play. We also smoked a cigarette or two back then. We had this club—it was a snake club to say the least. In order to be part of this snake club, we had to catch a snake and then snap its neck on the road and kill it. We then had to cut the snake up. There, done. We were now members of the snake club. Cool, man. I struggled really hard to become a member of this club. I wanted with all my might to show Brian that I was cool just like the rest of them. I did it, but I didn't like it. Was this peer pressure and trying to fit in back in the 70's? I guess so.

Horsing Around

When we lived at Willow's farm, my dad bought a horse. He was beautiful. His name was Beauty, and he was a mean son of a bitch. Beauty used to bite anyone that came near him. I'm not real sure how old we were, but my dad had my brother Andy try to ride this crazy horse. We all were scared of him, and I think Dad was too. So, this day my brother tried to ride the horse. Needless to say, he wasn't very successful. The horse bucked him off and was loose in the yard. Our neighbor Daniel came to help catch Beauty, and he did. Daniel was more familiar with horses and tried with all of his might to tame and calm Beauty down but was unsuccessful. Dad ended up selling Beauty because he was of no use to us being wild-spirited like that.

I'm a Little Teapot, Short and Stout

My first memory of school was when I was four years old. They called it Head Start back then. Head Start was held in the basement of the Baptist Church. I loved going to school. My friend Ellen also went to the school. Ellen's mom was my mother's best friend. I remember the wooden kitchen that we had to play with at Head Start, and I remember our cubbies to put our coats and hats in. My teacher, Mrs. Silvia, was kind and gentle. I remember the first song that I ever sang—"I'm a Little Teapot." I loved this song, and I practiced being a teapot; I was probably quite cute and obnoxious with repeating it over and over. It's strange the fond memories you carry with you into adulthood.

No Tricks, No Treats

For Halloween when I was probably six years old, we all decided to dress up like hoboes, but not just any hobo. We dressed it up a little, and we put cocoa powder on our faces after we put lotion on. The cocoa stuck to our faces, and we looked like little black hoboes. We had ripped blue jeans or overalls on, and we had red bandanas on our heads; we carried sticks with white rags with stuffing in them. The only house I can remember going to was my great grandparents' house. Why would I remember this house only?

Well, we got there and knocked on the door. We knocked and knocked. My great grandmother had a small diamond-shaped window in her wooden door. After knocking for what seemed to be forever, I saw my great grandmother's head peek out the window. She saw all five of us, her own great grandchildren, standing anxiously waiting for her to open the door so we could get some trick-or-treat candy. Nothing. She would not open the door to these "black" children. I couldn't believe it. We all were screaming, "Gram, it's us." There was no convincing this old-fashioned woman to open the door even for "these" little black-faced children. That is a Halloween I will never forget.

Hot-Blooded

My best friend Ellen and I spent a lot of time together in school and out. I loved to go to her house to play. She had a house full of brothers and sisters, and they seemed like a wonderful loving family. Ellen had a swing set out back, and I couldn't wait to play on it. I remember all the old cars and trucks in the yard. Nowadays, being an adult, I would think of it as a messy yard with junk everywhere. I used to love the old trucks and cars they had. We would get in them and play for hours. You would, however, have to be careful of snakes that would get in them. I remember being so small I would sit in the steering wheel and turn the steering wheel with my butt. It was the greatest. Ellen's dad had the meanest dog ever. Shelbie was a long-haired German shepherd mix. She was tied in the old barn off the side of the house. I peeked in the crack of the barn door once in a while, and all you could see was snarling, barking teeth.

I used to love to play and sing and dance with Ellen. We would go to her bedroom, one of many in her huge house. She shared a bedroom with her sister Kathy. Kathy was a year or so older than Ellen and me. Ellen had a cool record player. It was in a case that would close and had a fastener on it so you could lug it with you. My favorite song back in the day was "Hot-Blooded." Ellen and I would sing and dance to this over and over. One night while Mom and Dad were visiting and drinking downstairs, we were getting a little excited with our singing and dancing. We were dancing on the bed and jumping up and down.

I was scared to death of Ellen's dad, Ted, because he loved to holler and scream. I think he did it just to hear himself do it. No one ever really listened to him. So, Ted came crashing into the bedroom. He had the broom in his hand, and he was pissed. He had asked us a dozen times to turn down the music and to stop jumping on the bed. I just froze. I had no idea he wouldn't beat us with the broom. I just waited, and nothing. He continued to scream and holler, and then, poof. He was back downstairs. My heart didn't beat for a few minutes after that, I tell you.

Stop—Don't Stop

As my memories come in clips like an old black-and-white movie, I try to remember more of the details. My childhood traumas keep me from doing just that. I write and remember. Then I feel the fear, pain, sadness, or joy, and then I try to accept it and heal myself. It may not be today or tomorrow, but it will get better. The healing, no matter if it is an open wound or internal scare of the memory or your heart, takes time. If you slip and fall by relying on food, alcohol, drugs, sex, or obsessions, get right back up and try it again. That is the way we humans have had to do it since birth.

Bits and Pieces

It comes and it goes like a flash in the night.
I only get bits and pieces, never the whole of anything.
Why can't I remember?
Why do these memories fade in and out?
They are like clips from an old black-and-white movie—
No color, no sound, no feeling;
Just bits and pieces can be found.
I search my heart, and there is no beat.
My brain stands still as I try to think.
Bits and pieces—where is the whole of anything?
The hole I feel is within me.
Until I reveal the broken bits and pieces, I will not be whole.
I ask my father, from where you are, help me
To remember
These tiny bits and pieces.

Mom & Dad

CHAPTER 4

Mom and Dad's Story

To get my mother and father's story, I went to the source. Not every story can be told through the writer's experience or memories. The following is straight from the horse's mouth.

Mom and Dad met for the first time at the Grange Hall, where dances were held on Saturday nights. When they met it was not your traditional "hi, how are you?" meeting. It was the kind of meeting where Dad was on one side of the Grange Hall, and Mom was standing in the corner on the other side. They saw each other, and the attraction was there; their curiosity was piqued. Nothing else happened that night other than them knowing—knowing that he was there and she was there. Who was this handsome, quiet, shy man that stood surrounded by his rowdy friends? He noticed her slender-framed body and bright smile.

It wasn't until a few weeks later that Mom was on the dump road with her brother Harry. Mom and Uncle Harry were in a white 1950 convertible. As they were on their way out of the dump road, in drove Dad and his gang of rowdy friends—James, Paul, and Marvin. As Mom and Uncle Harry headed out of the dump road, Mom waved frantically to get Dad's attention.

When Mom and Uncle Harry arrived home, Dad and his buddies drove in. Dad was too shy to ask Mom out, so James asked Mom if she would go to the movies with Dad. Mom said yes, and it all started there. Their first date was a night at the drive-in movies watching *Jack the Ripper*.

Mom was seventeen, and Dad was twenty-three when they met. Dad didn't have a car, so they would always go with the gang. They would go out to his grandparents' camp swimming. They would pick Mom up after school to go riding around. Mom met all of Dad's friends from around town. They had fun for a very short time.

Mom ended up proposing to Dad. Dad was way too shy, and Mom, an outspoken woman, wanted this man. She wanted my dad to marry her. They dated from May 1960 to July. On July 9, 1960, Mom and Dad were married by the justice of the peace. They had their friends James and Linda stand up with them when they got married. They had a good-size reception at the town hall after they got married. During the reception Mom's friends Morgan and Paula "stole" the bride and drove around town. Paula screamed out the window, "We stole the bride," all through town. Mom said this was called a shivaree. It was common practice back then to steal the bride or groom. They ended up at the dance hall. Dad ended up joining them shortly after Mom arrived, and they danced and had a wonderful time.

Mom and Dad went to my great grandparents' camp for their honeymoon night. Mom only had her dress and high heels to wear at camp. She remembers having homemade canned meatballs for breakfast. It was rumored and believed that Mom and Dad got married because she was pregnant. Mom had a few disagreements with some people, and even though my oldest sister wasn't born until May 4, 1961, many people still believed it to be a "need to get married" scenario.

I remember my dad taking pride in any vehicle that he had. We have picture after picture of the vehicles that he had throughout the years. My mom tells me Dad's first vehicle was a 1950 black Ford. She remembers it because it had a bad steering rod. When you drove it to turn a corner, you had to turn the steering wheel around three times to get the vehicle to turn. She said it was actually quite dangerous to drive. Mom tells me that Dad's favorite vehicle was a 1966 white Plymouth with red interior.

Mom remembers Dad's first job was at a cedar mill in the town that he grew up in. I remember this mill. When we had animals, we used to go to get wood shavings to use for bedding for the animals. I remember how I loved the smell of the shavings.

Dad found a job working at a chicken house. Dad would clean the coops and lug the chicken feed bags. Dad would lug two 100-pound bags at a time, one on each shoulder. "That is how your father got built up," Mom told me.

When Mom and Dad first got married, they lived with Dad's mother. Mom hated every minute of it. She said Gram was not a good housekeeper at all.

Mom and Dad also lived for a short time with Dad's grandparents. The first home they lived in was a small camp. They lived next to Dad's Uncle Sean and Aunt Sally. The camp had dirt floors, and Mom remembers how cold the camp was. More of Dad's relatives lived right down the road from them. Mom remembers spending a lot of time with Dad's Aunt Lynn. Aunt Sally mentioned to my mother about her wondering why Dad's Uncle Evan couldn't stay with his own kind. Uncle Evan was married at the time to a Vietnamese girl named Sonja that he met and fell in love with while in Vietnam. After they were married, he brought her home to the States, and she wasn't very welcome in the family.

Mom worked in a shoe factory. She cut leather for shoes. This was a field of work that my mother would return to for many years to come. As Mom got older, she would work on the potato harvester to help get through the winter months.

Dad's first experience with driving truck started when he was twenty-four years old. There was a cement plant he worked at. Dad would move, park, and load the cement trucks while the other truck drivers went in to get alcohol. This was where Dad learned his love for driving truck. His first over-the-road job was hauling bagged cement on a flatbed. He then went to a cement truck mixer. Throughout Dad's career he worked as a cement truck driver, and he also hauled logs. He loved the early-morning and late-night shifts. Even after being on the road for twelve to sixteen hours a day, Dad would always find time for Sunday drives through the country and to visit with family, no matter how much he drove during the workweek.

Mom had five children really close together. As far as I am concerned, she did the best she could with the circumstances and times she was living in. Mom told me that all of her pregnancies went well. Mom remembers having to remind my dad that he had a family of his own, that he didn't need his family. She said this because of the way Dad's family treated him. They only wanted him around when they needed something done. That's how he felt while growing up and even as an adult.

Mom remembers her favorite things to do throughout her marriage with Dad. She enjoyed going to the dirt racetrack driving. She loved to dance at several of the local dance halls. She also enjoyed playing games with her older sister Janice and her grandchildren.

By Your Side

I stand with you by your side
Through richer, through poorer.
I stand by your side in the hardest of times.
I will love you forever.
I stand with you in sickness and in health.
I love you truly, I love you deeply.
I stand by your side to prove my love.
I love you until death us do part,
By your side forever.

CHAPTER 5

Where It All Began

Growing up you hear a lot of stories. It's sometimes hard to know what really happened. These pages are stories that I remember and stories that I've heard—stories from my mother, father, or my brothers and sisters, or even some that I have remembered. They say it's tradition to pass things down from generation to generation. Some things are better to stay in the past. There's no need to pass some things on. The following memories are just that, better left right where they started. That I believe is one big reason I have been so passionate to write my story.

I know from personal experience that my dad had an obsession with coming to my room and my sister's room to masturbate on a regular basis. He was even known to do it during the daytime while I was awake. I heard my mother tell stories of my dad before they dated that he was caught masturbating in the picture window of his mother's home while the schoolgirls went by. Yes, my mother knew that my father was a sick man before she married him. My mother still ignored and would not believe her own daughter when confronted years later with his sickness.

I know it's hard to understand how sick my dad was. After knowing all that my dad had put us through—the physical, mental, and sexual abuse—how could I forgive him? I have always been the one who tried to fix things, make things better, the healer of all hurts. After I had grown up and moved out of Mom and Dad's house and had my own children, I felt the urge to confront my dad and mom and my siblings. I felt the need to get all of our shit out on the table. Talk about it, hash it out, heal—and move on.

It was not an easy thing to do. To confront the man that you feared and hated and loathed and loved all at the same time. Everyone showed up for this confrontation, or healing if you will, except my sister Amy. In order to survive to the best of her ability, Amy had cut herself off from most of the family. Amy and I have still stayed in contact throughout the years, but each time the same things came up—the abuse, the lack of accountability, and the inability to forgive and move on.

As scared as I was to confront my dad that day, I knew I had to do it for myself and for my own children. We all sat around the table—Mom and Dad, Eva, Andy, Robert, and me. We talked about normal stuff—the grandkids and work and the weather. Then I got down to business. I confronted Dad about his masturbating and his abuse; I just wanted him to finally admit it. I wanted him to say he was sorry for all the pain that he had caused all of us.

My dad claimed that he could not remember doing it. He truly could not remember it. I could not comprehend at that time of our confrontation, how someone could do such a horrible thing and not remember doing it. After years of living with and trying to cope with my own abuse, it is more believable that just maybe he didn't remember it.

My dad did apologize that night to all of us for hurting us physically, and even though he couldn't remember doing it, he apologized for the sexual abuse. My dad was quiet and almost distant. He was slow with his responses, and he would stare at the table or at the dirty ashtray on the table that we all sat around. I don't ever remember my father looking as sad and distant as he did that night.

My father opened up about his childhood and some of the things that he had been put through. This in no way gives my father acceptance for his behavior or his choices with what he did to his own children. I hope to enlighten people to the importance of awareness of what's going on around you as a parent or caregiver. I also want everyone who reads this to know how devastating the choices you make can be on the lives of others. We as parents, grandparents, or family members in general all have the ability to prevent the abuse, whether it's sexual, physical, or emotional. It's our job to protect the lives of those who are too small or too afraid to help themselves.

My father talked about his mother, my grandmother Amy. The woman who in 1937 got pregnant out of wedlock and did not want to keep him. The woman who was supposed to love him and nurture him, yet let her own mother and father raise him. Was it because she couldn't stand the fact that she had screwed up and gotten pregnant? What would cause a woman to not love her own flesh and blood? How could she let her own parents raise him while knowing that was her son?

Dad told of his visits to his mother. She was cold and distant and unloving. Dad had a sister, Alice, and a brother, Jeff. Grammy Amy married Henry Thompson, a man I remember who sat in a green leather recliner. He couldn't talk, and I never saw him walk. I believe he had Parkinson's disease. I remember drool coming out of his mouth and snot coming out of his nose. Tissues, tissues were everywhere—on his table next to him, with his water glass, on his lap, and on the floor by his feet. When he did try to talk, it was like in a raspy whisper. I never could understand him. I felt sorry for him. I, as a child, wondered. What did she do to him? Why was he like this? It was just part of me being a child and not understanding the world that I was surrounded by.

My father told a story that was unimaginable, but how could you make up such a memory as that? My grandmother was unfaithful to Grampy Manly. Big shocker, I know. My grandmother would have her gentlemen friends come to the house, and she would have sex. While she was having sex, she would make my father, a small boy, watch. I can't imagine what would run through a child's mind. I remember with Dad's masturbating, I didn't have the slightest clue what he was doing. I just knew it was wrong and disgusting, and I had no idea why my father would do that to me.

My father for all the years that I knew him never felt loved by his own mother. He would never measure up to his brother or sister. My father was used by his mother and even his grandparents for manual labor. I remember Dad always dragging his feet to go visit because he knew they would always want him to mow the lawn, fix the roof, and fix the dock out to camp. Always something needed to be done. We got to go swimming when we went to camp, but that was the only good thing.

This is where the apple doesn't fall far from the tree. I believe I was nine or ten years old, and my great grandfather hadn't been in a wheelchair long. Up to this point I hadn't had any issues that I can remember with him. This day I learned quickly to stay an arm's length or better away from him, or he would grab your boobs or stick his cane up between your legs. That wasn't the worst of it. He would look at you and smile, almost as if to say, "How'd you like that?" I never thought the same of my great grandfather again after that day.

I only know what happened with my dad, and I only know what happened with my grandmother and my dad. My great grandfather was also a dirty old man. It truly makes me wonder what kind of hell he put my grandmother Amy through. Maybe even my dad.

Down through the generations, many things can be passed down and should be passed down. Like my mom's Bibles will go to my sister Eva. My sister Amy got my grandmother Gloria's special 114-year-old gold spoon, I got my mother's wedding ring, Andy got Mom's hutch, and Robert got Dad's guns. These are precious heirlooms to help connect us to the past. These are all things we will hold dear to our hearts no matter what our childhood was like.

To pass down abuses, however, is nothing more than acting like a wild animal out of control. No love for the young children is ever considered. When someone is subjected to such horrific acts of inhumanity, why do they pass it on and share it with the ones they are supposed to love the most? If nothing else, with my book, I hope to help people learn how to face their own demons and move on past their past, whether it be by seeking proper counseling or by writing their own journey and healing themselves through their own words and self-awareness. I have strived for the last nine years to heal myself. I have been to many counselors and holistic healers and psychiatrists, and it has all helped me to get through those moments where I didn't think I could go on another day.

If you're a victim of abuse or you know someone who is suffering from abuse—whether it is physical, emotional, or sexual—reach out. Reach out for help. Just let them know you're there for them, a shoulder to cry on. If it is a child, we have a duty to protect those who cannot protect themselves. There are hotlines that are anonymous to help protect you. I really wish my teachers back in high school would have intervened that day long ago when I was fifteen.

I also have learned from all that I have witnessed and experienced in my life that as hard as it may have been, someone somewhere had it worse than I did. I know that these were all part of my life's lessons. If I had not been subjected to this abuse, what kind of a woman would I be today? Would I be loving, kind, and giving? Would I have chosen to take care of the elderly most of my life? How would it have changed me as a mother? Would I have been a better mother, or would I have been worse for not going through the hardships that I did? Would I not be as compassionate and caring? I feel we all experience exactly what we are supposed to, to be stronger and better human beings in the end.

As sick and mean as my father was to his own children, he was a compassionate and loving grandfather and great grandfather. What changed him, I cannot say. Was it the fact that he had an epiphany one day and changed? Was it the fact that he had most of his children confront him and give him the opportunity to confess and to be forgiven? It doesn't matter why he changed, not really. It just matters that he did. If my dad can change, coming from the hatred and sickness that he grew up with, then I believe with all of my heart that anyone can change.

Stop the Madness

Hear my cry for the children who still suffer.

Year after year and generation after generation it continues.

Listen to them, watch them, save them from the animals.

We have failed for far too long; we have lost too many pure souls

Way sooner than was meant to be.

Stop the madness.

Save a child.

Be it

Sexual,

Physical,

Or

Mental,

The abuse has gone on far too long.

Hear their cries, hold them to you, love them.

We are meant to be their protectors,

Their mother, their father.

Stop the madness.

Dad age 4

CHAPTER 6

The Forgiving

It wasn't until many years later that I sat in my father's doctor's office with him and had my first real conversation with my dad. There were many events that led up to this point in my father's life. Dad was a workaholic, an alcoholic, and an abusive man. He had made many bad choices with his life. When I look back on his life, he was a hard worker. He woke long before dawn and worked long after dusk. He had five kids' mouths to feed and a wife to support. Growing up in all of the drama of sexual abuse and mental, emotional, and physical abuse, I missed a lot about my dad. After having three of my own children, I learned quickly that not all was bad where my parents were concerned. I will always remember my mother saying, "You kids didn't come with a handbook." I, like my mother, learned as I went along.

The year was 1996. I was twenty-nine years old, and I had seen more in my twenty-nine years of life than most young women my age. Living with all my childhood drama and working as a Certified Nursing Assistant for most of my life, I had seen the end of life's cycle more times than I like to remember. Dad's health was failing fast due to working too many hours, drinking, smoking, and life's stresses. Yes, men get stressed out just as easily as women.

Dad had been having heart attacks and ministrokes, for how long I'm not sure. It was affecting his memory and his ability to work as a truck driver. I remember him talking in the kitchen one day when he came home from work because he was unable to put chains on the tires of his truck. This he had done more than a hundred times. He told me about how he got lost for hours coming home from hauling a load of logs. He couldn't remember how to get home, and he was scared. I am glad that he decided that day to quit smoking. I believe that helped him to live as long as he did.

I remember feeling like time was ticking away. I felt like his days left on earth were numbered. I could sense Dad panicking, like he felt unsure of his future for the first time. So, when I took him to his neurological appointment, we were in the waiting room, and I had an overwhelming urge to talk to my dad.

Dad thanked me for bringing him to the doctor's.

I said, "No problem, Dad." In my need to clear the air before too much time passed, I just said it. "Hey, Dad, do you remember all the bad shit you have done?"

He said, "Yes."

I just said it. "I forgive you, Dad, and I love you."

My dad took a deep ragged breath, and he said, "I'm sorry, and I love you too!"

No more words; nothing further. That's how easy it can be. Forgiveness. Clear the air. Get it out there.

I've looked at my dad differently ever since that day. I knew in my heart that he was truly sorry. Yes, it took a scare with his illness and the threat of not knowing his future for him to say he was sorry. I'm glad we were able to have that conversation and were able to move on to the close relationship we shared from that point on.

I found my father to be an amazing grandfather. Sometimes it takes us screwing things up as parents to be able to see things through different eyes.

I remember the way Dad would be with my kids, and I just shake my head and grin. What a loving man he turned out to be. Father's Day is in twelve more days. It will be my first Father's Day without you, Dad. I will miss you greatly, but you better believe I will be listening to Patsy Cline or Charlie Pride, and I will remember all of the good things that you brought to my life and Mom's life and to my children. Thank you for helping me be the woman I am today.

R.I.P.

Andrew Allen Carter Sr.

September 6, 1937–August 28, 2013

Daddy's Little Girl

It seems so long ago, yet it has only been ten months.
I held your hand; we prayed your last rites.

It seems so unfair we never had enough time—
Time to sit, time to share.
I miss you, Daddy!

We all came to visit you, we laughed, we cried,
We grew. We knew the end was soon.

Quietly in the background Patsy plays your favorite tunes.
I knew, you knew.
Daddy's little girl.

So, you go out walkin'.
We will meet you after midnight.
Love you, Daddy's little girl.

June 2, 2014

My love of poetry for the first time in twenty-eight years was put to paper,
and I cried and I healed for the loss of my father.

CHAPTER 7

My First Crush

Brian was the boy next door. He had four siblings just like I did. Back in our day, we played outside or worked all day. The only time we were inside was to eat, take a bath, do chores, or sleep. If my brothers, sisters, and I weren't at Brian's house, then he and his brothers and sisters were at our house. We would build tree forts, go fishing, swim in the brook down the road, or go for walks. We also played touch football, which I didn't care for. I was the youngest and smallest, and I would always end up getting hurt. We would play ghost in the graveyard at night—which I hated. We also would catch lightning bugs and smear them on our shirts so we would light up and then play hide-and-seek. During the winter we would all get on the hood of an old car and slide down a huge hill. It was an old pit, and it had a pond right in the middle; we would all go flying down the hill and slide across the ice if we made it past the edge of the pond. If not, we all would end up stopping short and in an abrupt halt. We all would land on top of one another. It wasn't fun at all if you were the one on the bottom. Those were the good old days. Those were the good times in my childhood.

Yes, I had this huge crush on Brian, and everybody knew it. Teasing was the same back then as it is today. If someone knew something about you and it embarrassed you or made your life difficult, everybody made it known. Looking back on it now, I didn't mind it so much. Especially if Brian talked to me or paid attention to me. I just remember smiling and blushing.

It was fall one year, and hunting season had just gotten underway. It was one of those crisp cold days in New England that I love. Brian was new to hunting, and he and his friend Brad went hunting alone in the woods behind his house. It was getting dark, and Brian and Brad started fooling around like your normal teenagers would. They were spooking each other. Brian and Brad ended up running with loaded rifles. Brad tripped and dropped his rifle. When his rifle hit the ground, it fired. The bullet from Brad's rifle ricocheted off of a rock and hit Brian in the leg. When the bullet hit his leg, it hit the femoral artery. Brian didn't have a very good chance of surviving. They were way out in the woods, and daylight had already burned out. By the time Brad, family members, and the rescue crew arrived, it was too late. Brian had bled out and died, my first of many young lives to be taken from this world. A life snatched away like a thief in the night. Gone from me forever.

Over the next few days, I remember all the commotion and drama. Tears, anger, and blaming. I was confused. I had never dealt with this death thing before. In the 70's, in my house kids were to be seen and not heard. I don't remember how many times my father had spoken those words. To share emotions, especially when you were hurt or sad, was unheard-of.

When I went to Brian's funeral, I got it real quick. I learned everything about death, except how to cry. I wouldn't allow myself to feel the pain, to let him go. As I walked to the door of the funeral parlor, the first thing I saw was lots of people. People I didn't know. There were a few people I did recognize. Everyone was either crying or talking or just staring off into space. The closer I got to the door, the more I heard this funny music. It kind of sounded like the music you hear at church. It was just so slow and so sad. The feeling of sadness that I already had got even worse.

As we were greeted coming through the parlor, I felt sick to my stomach. Like someone had rammed me in the stomach with their big fat head while playing football. I could smell old ladies' perfume, and then something else hit me. I didn't recognize this smell. It wouldn't be until years later that I knew what that smell was. Even today I hate the smell of a dead decaying body.

I don't remember my parents being there. They must have been. I only vaguely remember my brothers and sisters being there. I played this over in my mind many times over the years. The loss of my beloved crush. To me, it was like Brian and I were in the parlor alone. No one else was present. The reverend was speaking. I do not remember the words he said.

When I first saw my first crush, Brian, lying in his brown coffin, the rest of the world did not exist. I noticed immediately that he was wearing his brightly colored two-piece suit. Only Brian could pull off wearing a fuscia-colored suit. It suited his playful personality to a T. That was one of the reasons I loved him so much. He had his eighth-grade pictures taken in that suit, and that is how I remember him. I will never forget how handsome he looked. I stared in disbelief. I thought, *he's gone. He's really gone.* There was a knot in my stomach. I didn't understand that feeling. I didn't realize the tears that I held back would be just the beginning of how I had learned not to deal with my emotions. I didn't know the trouble I would face in the years to come from not experiencing the emotional process that someone should go through after losing a loved one.

That was just the beginning for me and the death that I would experience. With each death comes more shock, horror, and disbelief. How can a God so good let such horrible things happen? As I got older and experienced more death, I came to understand and experience things beyond the imagination with death. I finally understood the loss of a loved one. I understood the process of birth, the short or long life we live here on earth, and the death that follows.

I may have lost my first crush all those many years ago, but I look forward to seeing Brian in the afterlife. To renew a friendship with Brian is just one of the gifts that I know God will allow me to experience when it is my time to cross over. Until we meet again, Brian. All my love, Bella.

Innocent Love

We met at a very young age.

We became friends. We played. We explored life's wonders.

You were just being a boy, a boy who was full of life.

It was your time. Time to teach. Time to move on.

Your new path had been set in motion.

The pain you left behind was tremendous.

How do we go on? How do we grow? How do we accept this?

I have missed your beautiful smile and your innocent energy that was infectious.

I will be patient. I will hold on. I will love you yet again.

It is young innocent love that goes on and on.

Until then, my dear friend, we will meet again.

Chapter 8

First Love

Growing up back in the 60's, 70's, and 80's and coming from the background that I did, there wasn't much room for dating. My first date was a double date with my best friend Judy, whom I had known since I was five years old.

So, I was almost eighteen years old and had never been on a date. I had no clue about how a date worked or what was expected. On the other hand, it was an escape for me. I really wasn't interested in the guy that I was going out with. Oh, don't get me wrong; he was a real nice guy. His name was Johnathan and he was funny and lovable, but that was it. He sat next to me in history class. I think he was hoping for more. Being eighteen and a guy, it was the same then as it is today. Guys just want to have a really good time!

Not me—I just wanted to get out of the house. So, Judy and I planned on sitting in the backseat together. Which totally wasn't what the guys were hoping for. I don't even remember what movie we went to see. I just remember I was eighteen and going on my first date!

It wasn't until I was nineteen that I went on my second date, a blind date. I was set up on this blind date by my friend Jan. Since my first date didn't go so well, I was not looking forward to this one. My blind date's name was William. I was so reluctant to go that I arrived two hours late. When I finally got there, I was pleased with William's looks. He wasn't bad-looking at all, compared to the last guy—oh my! So, I ended up having a good night at the North Star, a local bar and dance hall in town. William and I hit it off well and had several more dates. William and I decided to move in together just a few short months after meeting. We lived together for about nine months, and he popped the question our first Christmas together. I of course said yes. My biological clock was ticking, and in those days, you graduated high school, got married, and had kids. It was that simple.

Things went well for William and me for a while, until we had children. Not that it was in any way the kids' fault for our being overwhelmed with finances or our lack of communication. As a mother of three and trying to keep a marriage together that was just falling apart at the seams, it was not easy. Not to mention my underlying bipolar issues that had not been diagnosed yet.

So, William and I rambled on through our marriage, and we grew and became just a little more disconnected over the years. I decided I needed something other than children and housework. It took William a lot of adjusting to get used to the changes that I went through over the years.

As I got more independent with having my life, I went back to college for a year and worked part-time as a cashier in our town. It was a hustle-and-bustle kind of life for all of us. Billy and Corey were in day care, and Ann Marie went to school.

After graduating college I decided to get work. I worked full-time at our largest and local mental health institute as a food service worker. I liked the staff that I worked with, but it just wasn't fulfilling for me. I missed my Certified Nursing Assistant work. I missed taking care of people, and I went back to work where I felt needed and loved. I went to work at our local veterans' home taking care of veterans or their spouses. It has always been a rewarding job for me.

The more independent I became with working, the more my compulsion to shop or buy things became an issue. The more money we would make, I would just spend it. It became a huge issue not just for William, but for us as a whole family. The kids were learning they could get most anything they wanted; with my guilt of not being there for them, I wanted them to have the things they wanted and the things I never had when I grew up.

So, spending more money than what was coming in was a big marital issue for William and me. It was one of the last things William warned me about. I was driving around yet again in a vehicle that was unsafe and would not pass inspection. I decided to shop around for a vehicle because I couldn't get William to fix the hunk of junk I was driving. I found the car I wanted. I tried to get him involved in the purchase of a new vehicle, but he was just not up for another payment. Needless to say, I got the van, even after William told me if I did, it would be over. He was so upset with me after my purchasing the vehicle, that's when we stopped talking to each other.

When I decided to start my own cleaning business in September 2000, I wanted to help support the family and build a better home for all of us. William wasn't on board with it for a long time. He went along with it, but he was always on a different page than I.

As I worked my ass off, literally working seventy to eighty hours a week, I missed so much with the kids. The more I worked, the further apart William and I grew. It was like we would meet at the door and not even acknowledge one another. A marriage can only survive for so long once the love has died.

William had been living his own life, and I was living mine. The stressors of our marriage and work and my underlying bipolar II surfacing were the nail to seal our fate.

In July 2006 was my first hospitalization for my mental illness. Then just fourteen months later, I again fell victim to another manic episode. Working copious hours a week, not sleeping, and my marriage falling apart were not doing my bipolar any good. The more stress I endured, the less sleep I got. I knew I would have to do something, or I would end up, yet again, in the hospital.

So, in March 2009 I decided it was time to take charge of me and my life. I couldn't take the anxiety of the way William's and my life was going.

My decision came after eight years of struggling. How would I make it on my own—and the kids, what would the kids think of their crazy mother? Ann Marie was in college, and William Jr. and Corey still lived at home.

The guilt of giving up was still there, as well as William's family blaming me for leaving. I sat on the opposite couch from him. It was just him and me. The kids had gone to bed. I had no emotions left. It was like I was dead inside. I said, "William, I want a divorce." I believe he was relieved that I took all the pressure off him. He was tired of fighting. He was tired of my bipolar, and he just wanted out.

William and I had some good times. We just let all of the crap, like so many people do, get to us. We never loved each other enough to be supportive of each other. We did not communicate at all. We just ambled along for twenty-three years. I tried to pretend it would all work itself out.

A Love Is Lost

When we first met, I was so taken by your good looks.
Your charm and your laughter had me hooked.
We danced and we talked until last call.
The courtship was exciting and new to you and me.
I was your first and you were mine.
Maybe it went too fast. Did we really know one another?
The marriage, the children, and then time just
Whirled by both of us.
No time for you, no time for me, it slowly slipped
Through our hands, a love lost to fear, anger, and time.
Some love was never meant to be, just for a glimpse of time.
A love is lost, yours and mine.

Ann Marie, Corey, & Billy

Ann Marie & Corey

Billy & Ann Marie

CHAPTER 9

Motherhood

I wasn't married very long before the doctors told me that, because of my endometriosis, I would need to try to get pregnant. I might not be able to get pregnant in the future if I didn't try now. It wasn't a very hard decision for me to make. I had known for a long time that I wanted to have children.

William and I tried to get pregnant a little over nine months. We tried all of the tricks. We tried to elevate my pelvis after sex. We tried timing it so many days after my cycle ended. We also tried taking my temperature and racing around to have sex when my temperature was just right. Then, finally, we were pregnant. We were going to have our first child. What a happy time for both of us.

I loved Ann Marie from the moment of conception. It was an undeniable bond from the get-go. I enjoyed every pound gained and every kick late at night. I guess the morning, noon, and night sickness I didn't like so much. I remember having a package of saltines at the head of my bed and snacking on them at the wee hours of the morning.

My pregnancy with Ann Marie went well, other than being sick for four months. During the last few weeks of pregnancy, she decided to turn. The doctors had to schedule a C-section for the safety of the baby and myself.

Yes, Ann Marie decided that she wanted to come into this world feet first and stand tall. She's been standing tall and proud ever since.

On January 31, 1990, I was lying on the operating table with my guts cut open. The doctors asked my husband, "What do you think?" and he told the doctor, "It's not any worse than gutting out a deer." He always had a way with words!

So, we had our first miracle, Ann Marie Allen. She was named after her Aunt Ann Marie on her dad's side, who had been killed by a drunk driver when she was just five years old.

Ann Marie has always been like a sponge—quick to absorb all the information around her that she could. Ann Marie's dad and I are extremely proud of her. She grew up too fast. Helping take care of her younger brothers and being the old soul that she is, she took care of them like they were her own offspring.

Ann Marie is smart and beautiful. I could say that her father and I did a great job of raising her, but this is where I have to give her the credit for being the wonderful woman that she is today. I believe that if it wasn't for her ability to escape in her music and her artistic abilities, she would have had more of the same issues that I have. I think Ann Marie learned how to handle stress and anxiety to the best of her abilities.

With my second child, I did not have to try very hard to get pregnant. William and I knew we wanted more children, and we sort of just got pregnant. We were very happy to be having another child. The pregnancy went well. There were no complications. The doctor, however, did decide on another C-section. He stated that the baby's head was presenting to be large and for safety's sake it would be best to schedule a C-section. So on January 29, 1993, our beautiful baby boy William Aaron Allen Jr. was born. He was named after his dad. He weighed a whopping nine pounds two ounces, and he was so perfect. We ended up having Ann Marie's birthday party in the hospital. Their birthdays being only a few days apart has been a challenge for many years. Billy was a really good baby. It wasn't until I had my third child and he was just two years old that I noticed he was having behavioral issues. I was in turmoil of my own, dealing with undiagnosed bipolar, surfacing childhood trauma, and a marriage that was not doing well, and I was unprepared to raise three children with all of these other issues surfacing.

I look back now and wish I had known how to ask for help so that my children wouldn't have had to suffer with anxiety and depression. My poor Billy ended up in the very same hospital that I had spent three stays in. Yes, Billy was diagnosed and hospitalized for mood disorder, psychosis, and psychosocial stressors when he was sixteen years old.

When Billy was just two years old, he would bang his head on the floor whenever he was mad or frustrated. He also had an extremely hot temper. I remember chasing him around our house, trying to catch him. He would take any sharp object and try to stab or poke his brother or sister with it when he was angry. These outbursts got so bad I took him to a counselor, but Billy would not talk to the counselor. He would just laugh at the counselor when asked questions. The counselor decided that Billy would not open up to him and the sessions would be useless. If I had only been of a better frame of mind, if I was a better-prepared parent, maybe I could have helped him more.

One late night back in April 2009, William and I were watching TV, and we heard a knock on our front door. It was a police officer. My mind was racing, wondering what he wanted. He asked if William Aaron Allen Jr. lived here and if he was home. We said, "Yes," he was downstairs in his room. The officer stated that Billy had been sending concerning text messages to a friend of his, and his friend was worried that he might hurt himself. After getting this information from the officer, we went to Billy's room to confront him.

We learned through Billy's stay at the mental hospital that he had been hearing voices. A male voice was telling him that no one loved him and that he (the voice) was the only one that cared about him. The voice wanted Billy to kill himself. We also found out that he had been hallucinating and seeing bugs, and we were already aware of Billy's night terrors and sleepwalking.

Billy had a plan to kill himself one day after school. Billy planned to take one of his father's guns and kill himself. He said the day he planned to kill himself, we came home and interrupted his plan.

We found out that he would come home from school and get into his father's alcohol supply and drink two or three drinks nightly. I believe he was drinking to help cope with the stress of family life and try to escape his hallucinations. Billy's dad could be a bit harsh with expectations and seem harsh with his punishments. There wasn't any violence per se, but the emotional and mental abuse was definitely an issue. I believe Billy was also trying to escape the voices in his head.

Billy got on medication and had therapy treatments for a while, but in his efforts to not be a burden to his family, Billy decided not to continue with his medications. His medication alone was going to cost $700.00 a month, and Billy would not have that added expense for the family.

Billy met his first girlfriend shortly after his hospitalization. She seemed to help him out a lot. She helped him focus on love and life, and he has done well ever since. He has turned into a wonderful young man. Billy has been at the same job for over five years. With me being diagnosed with bipolar, I know from my own experience that if you're not compliant with your medications, there will be a relapse. Maybe not right away, but when you least expect it. I do have concerns for his mental health, but he is a young man and I have never been able to make him do anything that he didn't want to do. So, I pray that God watches over him and that if he ever needs help, he will come to me.

Pregnancy with our third and final child was a little more stressful. Billy of course was just little when I got pregnant. I was having issues with being uncomfortable carrying the new baby just a few months into the pregnancy. However, I carried him to full term. The doctor wanted me to have another C-section because I had two previous C-sections. The scheduled C-section was for December 27, 1994. Yes, Corey Robert Allen was born just two days after Christmas and just two years shy of Billy's birth.

After Corey's birth things were rough from the get-go. I ended up spending twelve additional days in the hospital on top of the seven days after my C-section. I was having some difficulties with infection, and Corey was not thriving well with my breast milk. The doctor and I decided to bottle-feed him, which would help me to heal better and faster. It would also help Corey to gain the weight he needed to be able to go home. The doctors tried to keep him from me when I went back to the hospital because of my infection and high fever. They thought it would be better for me to send my baby home with his father. I in no way would let that happen. I had three different types of staph infection. I ended up with drain tubes, and I was under a tremendous amount of stress. Corey was a fussy baby, and Billy was beginning to have more than your normal terrible-two behaviors.

I was so unprepared for all that would unfold. Billy just starting with his behavioral issues. The demands of another baby, and this baby being more demanding than either of the other two children ever were. My marriage was getting worse, and I still had not been diagnosed with bipolar.

Corey was a beautiful baby. He was, however, demanding from the get-go. I was not ready to handle two children so close together as Billy and Corey. Poor Billy was always pushed to the side. Always asked to give up his toys to Corey, so he wouldn't cry. Ann Marie was made into a five-year-old mommy. She helped me out with both of the boys. She did it so easily. At least I thought it came easily to her.

Corey ended up later on having some learning difficulties. He was never diagnosed with any learning disabilities. Corey kind of fell in between the cracks. As he got older, he became more difficult with behaviors, anger, swearing, and literally causing fistfights with his brother, Billy. It got to the point where I was going nuts. I was diagnosed in 2006 with bipolar. In 2009 I had Corey evaluated for his anger and his learning disabilities. He was diagnosed with anxiety and depression. He went to counseling for almost two years. It helped him tremendously. He got better grades in school, and he was learning how to handle his anger differently.

Corey moved into my trailer after my divorce, but it only lasted a few days. Corey and Billy ended up in a knock-down, drag-out fight in the driveway of the trailer park. Corey decided to move back with his dad, which was extremely difficult for me. I not only felt like I had failed at my marriage, but I was also failing as a mother. I knew in my heart of hearts that I would not be able to handle too many of those kind of fights like we used to have on a daily basis while living with his dad. So, Corey moved back with his dad. I saw him as much as I could.

Corey is now doing wonderfully. He has a good-paying job working for a plumbing company and loves his work. His dad and I are proud of all that he has accomplished.

My children enjoyed all the activities that other children do. Ann Marie started in Brownies in kindergarten and went through all the steps to a girl scouts until she was in her late teens. She enjoyed the friendships, summer camp, and traveling. She went to New York, Washington, and even Ireland. Ann Marie has a natural brilliance about her. She is book-smart and artistic and has grown into a wonderful woman.

Billy has a natural ability to just love. He has his group of friends. Whether he was playing baseball or football, he put his whole heart into the game. His dad and I were never more proud of him than the year he won Grand Champion Reserve. All three of the kids raised a lamb. He got Lilac shortly after she was born. It his first year in 4-H, and I never saw Billy more excited than he was that day.

Corey always loved to be on the go. He would help anybody, especially if they would give him something to eat. He loves sports like his brother. Corey seemed most interested in his wrestling and football. He was the quarterback of his team, and even though their team didn't win many games, he played his heart out.

Motherhood has been a wonderful experience for me. I love all three of my children equally. I would do anything for them. There are many things I wish I could change, go back and undo the things I messed up, but then they wouldn't be the wonderful adults that they are today.

If there is one thing I have learned in life, it is that your life molds you into the person God meant you to be.

Mother of Mine

You are mine, Mother,

Kind and gentle, loving and forgiving,

Always fun, even though you were on the run.

Mother of mine,

There will never be another.

The stories at bedtime are memories I take with me.

Mother of mine, there will never be another like

This mother of mine.

CHAPTER 10

Depression

Depression—you hear about depression everywhere. It's like the diagnosis comes with every patient that has a bad day. There are several levels and layers of depression. There are numerous reasons that people suffer from depression.

I have learned through my own experience that depression can be paralyzing. You can be going about your day-to-day life, and it can hit you like a Mack truck. Depression can stop you in your tracks.

Thinking back, I remember my first bout of depression. I was in my teens, and I now know that I had every right to be depressed. I would go for days, and all I wanted to do was sleep. I had no appetite and no desire to be around people and do my normal everyday routine. Living in my house growing up, there was no room for what you did or didn't want to do.

I remember my first thoughts of suicide. I knew I wouldn't be able to live the way I was with the physical, sexual, and emotional abuse that I was enduring at that time. I was miserable, and even though I had friends and I could talk to them, it just wasn't enough. I felt like my miserable way of living would go on forever.

I was pretty new to the idea of killing myself. I would think about different ways to do it. I would fantasize about my funeral and who would be there. Who would miss me, if anyone? I would find myself crying as I lay in bed and fantasized about ending my own life. To stop the pain, the fear, the sadness, and the loneliness.

As I got older and moved on with my life, you would think that the suicidal ideations would stop. You would think my life would be better. My father could no longer abuse me. So, what was wrong with me? Why did I continue to have these crippling bouts of depression? Why did I still feel overwhelmed with emotions of sadness?

Throughout my marriage I continued to have bouts of depression. I would find myself sleeping whenever I wasn't working or tending to the kids. I had horrible episodes of complete out-of-control anger. Looking back, it didn't take a lot to provoke me.

I remember one incident when William and I were fighting. I was so angry and out of control, I couldn't stand to be in the house. I felt I had no place to go. I was always very good at slamming a door to get my point across that I was pissed. That night after screaming and fighting with William, I went out into the car and cried for what seemed to be hours.

My poor kids. This was just one of many episodes that they would witness their unstable mother having. I love my children with all of my heart and would move heaven and earth to make sure they are safe from harm's way. I know with all of my heart that my kids are the only reason that I never acted on any of my many suicidal ideations while I struggled with my depression, my bipolar, and our family dynamics.

My boys. I remember losing control. I had lost the ability to parent the way most mothers could. Corey, who was the youngest, demanded a lot of attention. He was very active and loved to play outside. He would beg his older brother, Billy, to go out with him, to no avail most of the time.

Billy started having behavior issues shortly after I brought Corey home from the hospital. William was two years old and would sit in the middle of the floor and bang his head on the floor. The scariest thing for all of us was when he would run around the house with any sharp object he could find. He had an extremely hot temper. He would try to stab Corey or his sister, Ann Marie, with knives, pens, or pencils. It didn't matter. If it was sharp, he would find it.

I would run after him and struggle to get whatever it was that he had. This was an ongoing struggle with Billy for quite a while. I didn't understand his behavior and never realized that he had any underlying issues.

As they got a little older, their fights got worse. They were bigger and stronger, and I had no control to stop their knock-down, drag-out fights. I would scream and plea for them to stop. Corey more than likely started the fight, and Billy would end it by hurting Corey.

I remember one day when my life was nothing but chaos. The boys were at it yet again. Fighting and screaming and carrying on. I lost it. I totally lost it. It's like I turned into this whole other person. I ended up picking Billy up out of the middle of the WWE match he was having with Corey. I threw him into the recliner that we had in the living room. At the exact moment I let go of him, I panicked. I knew at that instant that I had lost control. Still to this day, I cringe at the thought of what I did.

I'm not sure if my throwing Billy into the chair traumatized him more or the horrifying emotional outburst I had after I did it. I ran to my bedroom. I fell into my bed and cried. I cried the hardest that I have ever cried. I literally wailed like a baby. I couldn't stop. As the kids witnessed me having an emotional breakdown, they all three come into the bedroom to check on me. Ann Marie was probably six, Billy was almost three, and Corey was a little over a year old. I am aware of them coming into the bedroom, and my state of mind was not good at all. They came near the bed where I lay and cried uncontrollably. I remember looking up, and there stood Billy, big blue eyes and black long eyelashes. All he said was, "Momma," and then he smiled. I was crying, and as he smiled, I screamed at the top of my voice, "Go away." The kids had never seen me act like this before. They were so young and had no idea what was going on. I know now as I write this, my bipolar was in full swing, and I didn't even know it.

My depression would come and go. My suicidal ideations would go from taking medications or stabbing myself with a butcher knife, to looking for the perfect telephone pole or the biggest tree beside the road. I now know from seeing in the news and watching other people that had depression or bipolar tendencies, that just because you don't act on your suicidal ideations this time, it doesn't mean you won't next time. Anyone with mental illness having suicidal ideations, it is a matter of life or death and should be monitored closely by doctors and family members.

Where Did You Go?

Life is just a game. You know all the rules.

You've played this game a million times.

You forge through the abuse and survive.

How did you lose the only one you can count on?

Where did you go? How do you come back to the real you?

How do you know which is the real you?

As I play the game, the game of life, I will do my best.

I will take my piece and move it along this game of life.

Somehow I will look to You for peace and love.

I will find me with Your guidance. I will win this game of life, for I am a survivor.

CHAPTER 11

July 2006, Diagnosis: Bipolar II

Sometimes life seems to fly by and there's no way to stop it. I had been working seventy to eighty hours a week for about six years. My kids were busy going to school and doing their extracurricular activities in school and in 4-H and Boy Scouts.

My cleaning business was very successful. We had built a new house in September 2000. I was working my fingers to the bone trying to pay the mortgage and keep up with all the regular bills. We needed to pay for the kids' activities like wrestling and football and the trips to go with Girl Scouts to Ireland or New York. It was hard to keep up with it all. I felt guilty for not making it to most of the kids' functions. My business had to come first because that was what kept the kids in all their activities and having most anything they wanted.

I knew my husband was addicted to surfing the web and partying on Friday and Saturday nights. I was obsessed with his activities online, and I was like Nancy Drew when it came to checking his cell-phone calls from all of his little girlfriends. I would confront him, and the more I did, the less he cared.

William and I were just coexisting. We fought constantly, and he was drinking more and more. As I was getting overwhelmed with work, the kids were fighting like they were part of the WWE team, and there was nothing I could do to stop them. I was obsessing with William's obsessing over other women. I didn't even see my world crashing in around me.

At first I would listen to music. I was associating everything on the radio to something or someone in my life. I went six days without sleeping. The more I went without sleep, the less sleep I needed. I was running on pure adrenaline. It was like I had taken a jar of speed. I was writing frantically about everything. I would go through notebook after notebook. I just had to get all this down on paper. The songs, my thoughts, my fears—everything went into those notebooks.

After about three days of this, I called my sister Amy to come and get me. Amy took me to see her friend Marcia, who was a holistic healer and Reiki master. Marcia did a Reiki session on me and gave me a triple dose of valerian root, which should have knocked an elephant out. It didn't touch me.

When Amy and I got back to her house, I consciously tried to go to sleep, but I couldn't. I couldn't get my mind to shut off or my body to slow down. I was hyper and acted like a child. On day six William came to Amy's house to try to convince her that I needed to go to the hospital. Finally Amy agreed to let me go to the hospital with William. Shortly after that I found myself in the emergency room at the hospital.

I remember waiting way down at the end of the ER exam rooms, where the psych patients go. I saw a security man in the window of the door that was connected to the room. As William and I waited to be seen, I was still hyper and acting inappropriately. William had his work shirt on that had holes in it, and while I talked with him, I stuck my fingers in the holes of his shirt and ripped his entire shirt off him. There he stood in the ER shirtless.

The next thing I remember, the doctor came in my room and was talking with William. The doctor told me he wanted to give me a shot, and he asked me if I wanted it in the arm or the butt. I said in a whining voice, "But I don't wanna be shot" … and I then said, "in the butt." It was just seconds after the shot, and from then I remember nothing for two days!

I remember waking up two days later, tired and groggy and not knowing where I was. I remember being cold all the time; it was like they tried to keep us cold so we would be more alert. That's what I was thinking. They kept me drugged up. When I was awake enough to know where I was, I just wanted to go home. It seemed like the more I talked about going home, the longer they were going to keep me there.

I spent twelve days in the hospital trying to level my lithium level so my manic episode would come under control. They put me on Depakote for mood stabilizing and lithium carbonate to help with the chemical imbalance in my brain.

I remember attending classes for coping skills and counseling sessions and talking with the psychiatrist. I was trying to adjust to the medications that they were giving me, and I would constantly struggle to stay awake. I wanted to pay attention, to get better, to do what was expected of me so I could go home. I was just so drugged up.

I had one phone call when I was at the mental hospital. It was from a guy whose name was Charles Johnson. For the life of me I did not recognize who this was; I couldn't remember who he was. I got on the phone with him, and I had no clue who it was and hung up the phone. It came to me a couple of days later. It just so happened it was my best friend's husband, who had moved to California. I found out later that no one had called him to let him know I was sick or in the hospital. Charles just knew; he knew something was wrong, and he knew where to call.

I remember the kids coming to visit, and I remember coloring pictures with them. I did a lot of coloring and writing in my journal. I wrote letters to William, and I wrote letters begging to go home.

It was my first manic episode, and I later learned that your senses become more aware, more sensitive, when you are bipolar. The hospital had a piano in the recreation room, and I would sit and play one song over and over again. The same notes. The funny thing is, I don't know how to play the piano. The nurse on duty came in and told me he didn't know I could play the piano. I told him I don't. The nurse told me I was playing "Send in the Clowns." That just happens to be one of my favorite childhood songs.

After my twelve days at the mental hospital, I was able to go home. It was advised for me to rest and to attend outpatient therapy and to see a psychiatrist for medication management. They also had group therapy every week that the doctors thought would be helpful.

So, when I went home, I went to work that night. I attended only a handful of outpatient group sessions. I did, however, continue to see a therapist for medication management. William and I attended one group therapy session that was run by former patients with bipolar. William and I found the group to be unorganized; it did not have any structure. After our first visit, we never went back.

I think the biggest problem for William and me was the fact we never understood exactly what my diagnosis was, this bipolar II. What was it, and how do I live with it? The biggest key to understanding yourself and coping with your mental illness is self-advocacy; you need to know what you've been diagnosed with and how to treat it, and be compliant with your doctor's instructions for treatment.

Those steps I learned were just the beginning to taking care of myself. I know now it's not as black and white as knowing what the diagnosis is and how to treat it. Bipolar is a very unpredictable mental illness. I would experience two additional manic episodes before getting the full picture. If you don't succeed, try and try again!

Flying High

I drift in and out like a wave on the sand.

I go so fast I do not see the crash of the waves.

It hits me hard. I cannot rest; I must race the clock

To beat His plan. If I am steady and true, I can do it.

Flying high from the pace that I have given me,

They reel me in like a great white shark.

They can't tame this animal that I have created.

So on I fly to the next wave, until I crash again.

Chapter 12

Creativity and Me

Am I special? No. I feel I am unique in my own little nutshell! I have found enjoyment in reading and writing since I was in high school. In fact, English was the only subject I excelled in until I did nursing my junior year. I found journaling in high school to be an outlet for all of my anxiety and my teenage drama.

My first visit to the mental hospital in July 2006 was my first real insight into my creativity. While I was writing frantically about anything and everything, I knew even in my manic state that I wanted to write a book about my life and how my bipolar was impacting my life.

I feel my husband of twenty-three years feared me and my diagnosis. My children were not able to understand me and my disease. Bipolar is something that I knew very little about. In fact, before my diagnosis of bipolar in 2006, I knew nothing about it. I was in denial that I even had it until my third hospitalization on May 17, 2014, when I was hospitalized for ten days.

I knew I was crashing, and I needed help. This was the first manic episode that I realized I was actually in trouble. That rarely happens for bipolar patients; it is usually too late to catch yourself in the manic state.

My creativity has never been an issue for me. Everyone else, on the other hand, seems to fear it just a little. They don't realize that as long as I focus and channel my creative, enthusiastic, and passionate energies, great things can happen for me.

Is that what people fear—that I can actually be successful at what I want to do? I hope not, because I will never outgrow the people that stick by me and support me. These are the people that I want to be successful for. I want them to have faith in me and be proud of me. I want them to reap in the rewards of my hard work.

In history it is a fact that many talented artists were bipolar, including Florence Nightingale, Edgar Allan Poe, Jackson Pollack, Vincent Van Gogh, Virginia Woolf, and Ernest Hemingway. There is a strong connection with creativity for those suffering with bipolar.

It is theorized that these people are able to effect change in society because of the disorder of bipolar and the way people who suffer from it look at the world. They obsess to do positive changes in the world, to make a difference beyond everyone else's abilities or beliefs, and they obsess to make it happen. People with bipolar are known to predominately have higher IQs.

The great thing about bipolar and the people who suffer from it is that their creativity is an expression of therapy for them; for me my bipolar has been expressed in writing my own book, journaling and doing poetry, and running my own successful business—and having the desire and drive to make all of these things happen. I can personally attest to my creativity as being a wonderful thing, and I do not fear it at all.

Creativity

To play music,
To paint a mural,
To write a beautiful story—
These are all gifts.

Creativity is in all of us.
We must search.
We must find that drive.
We must unleash our own creativity.

We speak volumes through music.
We release our passion with paint.
We find ourselves with ink on paper.
Don't hold back the true you.

Create, live, love.
Be who you were meant to be.

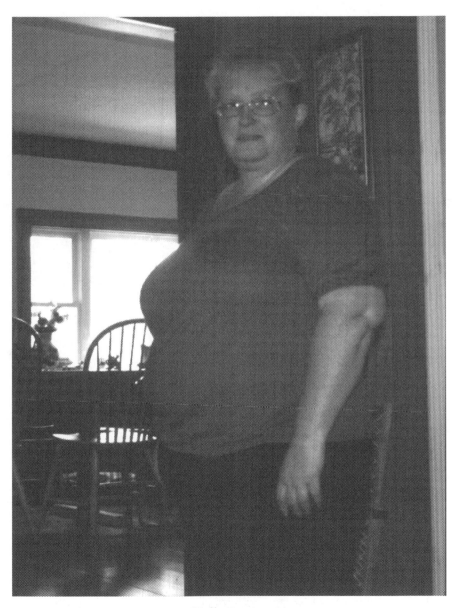

Bella Louise

CHAPTER 13

My Journey with Food

I have had a weight problem since I was in fourth grade. I started to "self-medicate," as they call it. I was living a life that no child deserved, and I had no way of knowing how to cope with all the abuse around me. I associated food with escaping. I felt I would focus on the taste, texture, and love of food. I would focus on anything other than the pain that went on in my head and in my heart and the reality that was going on in my life daily.

All through junior high and then high school, I was overweight. I had already developed many bad habits. When I got home from school, I would be so hungry from not having money to buy lunch, I would eat most anything I could find. I would eat peanut butter by the heaping tablespoons, butter right out of the dish, and brown sugar to fix a sweet craving. I was about forty or fifty pounds heavier than most of the other girls in school.

In my twenties to midthirties, I weighed on average around 220 pounds. That was of course obese for a five-foot-two-inch woman. I struggled daily with wanting to lose weight to keep my husband interested. But the food addiction was already well underway.

I would eat uncontrollably. I remember hiding candy bars and eating them when my husband, William, wasn't around. I would eat all the time while

I was cooking a meal, and then turn around and eat with everyone else at mealtime. It was a vicious cycle. I would eat to feel better, and then I would feel guilty for eating because I knew it was keeping me overweight. I would then start all over with the out-of-control eating.

I was diagnosed with bulimia and anorexia when I was in my twenties. I didn't know you could be fat and have anorexia. According to my doctor, you can. All you have to do is have the behaviors of starving yourself for days on end to qualify for anorexia. The bulimia I understood—I would eat out of control. Sometimes I would eat until I got sick. I even would try to make myself throw up.

A year after I had been diagnosed with bipolar, I had gained over a hundred pounds, which I definitely could not afford. My marriage was already in jeopardy, and my life was already compromised. I had high blood pressure. I was working an extremely physical job. I had sciatic nerve issues, and I was prediabetic. My health was failing fast.

I weighed 356 pounds at my heaviest. I was so unhappy and miserable. My self-esteem was next to nothing. I was journaling letters of self-hate all the time. I knew if I didn't do something and fast, I would not see my youngest boy graduate high school, and I wouldn't see any of my grandchildren be born.

The fall of 2012 I decided to have gastric bypass surgery. It was not an easy thing for me to admit I needed help. I needed it now. I had tried diet after diet and fast-fix remedy after fast-fix remedy for weight loss that there was. This time I knew I was in over my head.

I got signed up for gastric bypass surgery and went to all of my classes as scheduled. On March 12, 2013, I had my full gastric bypass surgery. Things did not go well at all. I did everything the doctors needed me to do—all the walking, all the drinking of clear liquids—and I went by all the rules. I went home when the doctor thought I was ready, and less than five hours after I was released, I was in an ambulance in excruciating pain. My abdomen felt like it was six times bigger than it was supposed to be. I could barely breathe. Just short, shallow breaths. I was sweating and extremely hot. The only words that came out of my mouth for the next six hours were "help me" and "Mamma." Over and over and over. I knew I was going to die. The pain was so bad, I just knew something terrible was wrong.

It wasn't until a few weeks after my surgeries that I remembered during my second surgery I was holding hands with a close friend of mine. He had recently died of a massive heart attack. Yes, my best friend's husband, Charles, and I were standing over my body holding hands. We were waiting. Waiting for me to die. Waiting for me to come back. There were no words spoken. Just the knowing of me making a decision. To stay or go. Since I am still here on earth, I guess God was not done with me here on earth yet.

What should have been a routine bypass surgery was not. I ended up having an abdominal leakage and a second surgery to repair the damage. Then I had five blockages, and the doctors had to go back in a third time—yes, three times in only four weeks—to widen and relieve the five blockages.

My doctor explained to me that the issues that I had with my surgery were uncommon; they also have hindered me in losing weight to the fullest benefit with the surgery. I was unable to go right back to work. My anxiety was extremely high, and I was unable to work and lost money. I almost lost my vehicle and my trailer. I was almost evicted. I was unable to take my medication due to the surgery, and I was very lucky not to have gone into a manic episode through that whole ordeal. Fear and stupidity kept me from telling anyone.

I did lose eighty pounds on my own before the surgery and have lost an additional one hundred pounds since the surgery. The surgery itself is not a miracle. It is only a tool to help lose weight. People can and do gain weight back after this surgery. I will have to be accountable for every morsel of food that goes into my mouth for the rest of my life. My days of compulsive eating have not disappeared. I battle with compulsive eating daily. I will need to love myself enough and control the stress in my life to prevent gaining the weight back. It will be a struggle for the rest of my life.

Escape

The fear of it all,
The hate of oneself,
The reasoning,

The lack of it,
The abundance of it,
The feel of it.

To live,
To die,
To escape.

The cycle one goes through,
The torture one feels.
No one understands.

Escaping with food,
Then right back where you started!
On and on and on!

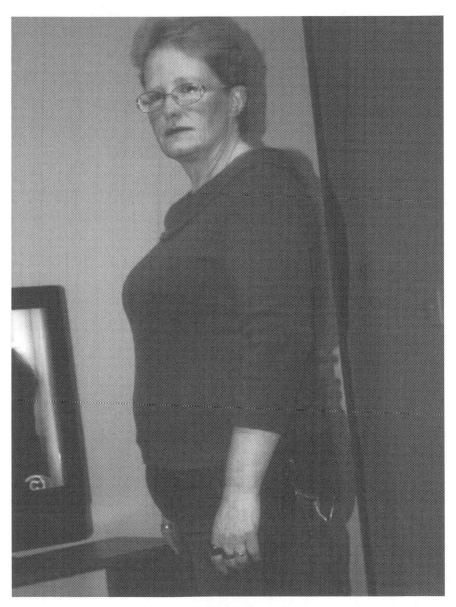

Bella Louise

CHAPTER 14

Death Is All around Me

I have seen death all around me since I was a child. I don't believe I have ever processed death the way they say in the books you should. There's denial, anger, mourning, and acceptance. I look back on my first experience with death and realize that at the age of nine, my process, not just with death but with every bad experience, was to shut my emotions off. It was a protective mechanism to continue to the next event (trauma) in my life or even just to make it to the next day.

As I went through my childhood, there were many deaths. People that I knew, and some that I barely knew at all. I lost more relatives and more friends of the family. Even though I should start to get used to the shock, disappointment, pain, and anger, it never really gets easier.

After graduating high school, I worked as a certified nurse's assistant, or for short, a CNA. If you're not familiar with the job of a CNA, we take care of the elderly, veterans, and handicapped. This work has impacted my life like no other job. Working as a CNA started my role as a caretaker, an empathetic, loving adult.

My first job as a CNA was in a local nursing home. I was in a different world when I walked through those glass doors at work. Most every patient that I took care of became my grandmother or grandfather. I will admit that there were those few special patients that I would take extraspecial care of. I would connect on a different level with them and bond with them.

The worst part of being a CNA was the inevitable circle of life. Eventually we all die. In a nursing home, you are surrounded by death. You get to know and love your patients. I used to see my patients, for the most part, more than I saw my own family.

Throughout the years that I worked as a CNA, I continued to shut out the pain that you're supposed to feel when someone dies. The one thing that I couldn't shut out was the pain that I witnessed from the patients or from the family members. I would feel their pain, but not experience my own grief. I had not one tear for myself.

I remember caring for my dying patients, taking their vital signs, turning them from side to side to prevent bedsores, swabbing their mouths with cool water, and changing their Depends. I remember giving extra time to make sure the family's needs were met.

The worst part ever of taking care of these beautiful frail people—people who shared their sad stories or their stories of love and accomplishments—was watching them die. It was like a part of you died every time another one was taken.

After a patient died in a nursing home, it was the job of the CNA to do a final check. We would have to call the charge nurse in to "call" the patient's death. We then would have to clean our patient from head to toe, a complete bed bath. After the bath we would put on a clean night gown and then put a toe tag on. The toe tag would have the patient's name and our facility's name on it. This would help funeral home to identify the patient.

One time while I was doing my routine of final care on one of my patients, I was freaked out totally. Cleaning up someone after he or she has passed away is creepy enough, but some of the things that you hear or feel or see, it's stuff that might come only from a really good horror film. I had a routine of always closing my deceased patients' eyes. It is much easier to clean them up if they are not staring at you with their cloudy gray lifeless eyes. While cleaning one frail-framed old gentleman, I closed his eyes. When I turned him back toward me after washing his back, "pop"—his eyes were open wide. I totally freaked out and got the willies up and down my back; I literally couldn't breathe. I was never scared of a dead body until that moment.

I continued to learn to shut the pain and tears off when someone I loved died. I dealt with more of my childhood trauma. I had a family that I lost myself in, and my life spun out of control with eating, anxiety, and the eminent bipolar disease that I had not yet been diagnosed with.

Almost a year later, my daughter lost her best friend. I had come home from work, late as usual, and my husband gave me the most unbelievable news ever. My best friend in the whole world, Carol, had lost her daughter Chelsey. She was in a car accident and died. Chelsey and her boyfriend died together. Just like that, I was numb. My mind was blank … Still there were no tears, just disbelief. It was shortly after my first bipolar manic episode that Chelsey died. I was still trying to get used to the medications for my bipolar.

I ask myself daily, why didn't I call Carol? The guilt I felt was beyond any I had ever known. The fear of what to say. I wasn't sure I could handle talking to Carol, let alone seeing her. I couldn't imagine how much pain she was in. I didn't want to think about it, I didn't want to feel it, and I didn't want to face it.

I believe this was the first funeral we went to as a family. I was like in a numb state. I remember just staring into space, and my mind was blank until I walked down the aisle of the church, knowing I would see my best friend in her worst moment of life. The loss of a child must be like God stabbing you in the heart and telling you, "I love you," at the same time. How does he give you such a beautiful gift as the life and love of a child and then snatch it away from you?

The closer I got to where Carol was sitting, the more I couldn't breathe. The knot in my stomach was unbearable. My head was spinning from the fear, and thoughts were running through my mind. "Oh, God, what do I say? There is nothing I can say to make this pain go away." When I reached Carol, she sobbed out loud and grabbed me, and I grabbed her. We did the only thing we could do. We cried and held each other until forever it seemed. No words were said.

Testing, testing, one, two, three. Yet again our faith was being tested. I started to wonder and I started to see a pattern and I started to get the picture. Another child, a very close friend of the family. My godmother's daughter, Theresa, lost her baby girl, Angela, at the age of five! Of all the people in the world to lose a child. A young woman with faith never-ending.

It wasn't until the death of my father that I understood the whole process that a loved one goes through and how a family can grow and get closer from losing a child, a mother, a father, a brother, or a sister. I had witnessed death and the process since I was nine years old. I never really got the entire process until I went through the painful process with my father and my family.

My dad had been sick for a long time. Over twenty years earlier, he started suffering from heart attacks and TIA's. He was an over-the-road truck driver. I remember him standing at the counter and being beside himself. He didn't know what he was going to do. Dad had been having trouble remembering things and how to do simple things that he had done for years—like getting lost coming home from a haul and not being able to remember how to put chains on the tires of his eighteen-wheeler.

This was just the beginning for my dad. He was diagnosed with Alzheimer's (which I don't think he had); I believe he had memory loss due to his TIAs and heart attacks. Even though he quit smoking, he still ended up having bypass surgery. Dad's diabetes ended up getting worse; he of course was not very good about staying out of food he wasn't supposed to have. It was a constant battle for Mom.

As Dad's diabetes got worse, he had to have dialysis. To me that meant the beginning of the end. I had been in the medical field enough to know it wasn't a good thing. Over the next few years, Dad was in and out of the hospital, scare after scare. We all knew one of these times he wouldn't make it out.

In August 2013, Dad went in the hospital for the last time. Dad's kidneys couldn't pump the fluid off his organs fast enough. He had also gotten an infection in his blood, called sepsis. Deciding to stop treatment was a hard decision to make, but it was an even harder thing to tell my dad. Dad didn't always understand everything you tried to tell him, so that was a challenge. I must say Mom did a super job explaining that the doctors had done all they could for him with his dialysis and there wasn't anything more they could do. She told him that they wanted to stop the dialysis and he would eventually go to sleep.

I cried and Mom cried when the only question he asked was, "Who's gonna take care of your mother?" I told him, "We will." Meaning the kids. A few minutes passed, and I could see him thinking. Then he asked, "How long will it take?" My dad was asking how long it would take for him to die. I can't imagine what he must have been feeling right then. He had been so scared of dying for so long. I wanted to just hug him and hold him, but I couldn't do that; I would have lost it. I needed to be strong for him and especially for Mom.

The next day everyone came to visit and spend time with Dad—Mom, Eva, Amy, Andy and his wife, Tricia, Robert and his wife, Sally, and myself.

Dad had been unresponsive since noontime. We talked and laughed like we had never done before as a family. I had brought in my radio and his favorite CDs—Patsy Cline, Charlie Pride, Elvis, and a few others. We listened to music. As time went on, Dad got weaker and weaker.

We all sat around Dad. He moaned a couple of times, and then he would be peaceful. We watched Dad and talked—when all of a sudden, his right hand and arm came off the bed. It was like someone had hold of it. His back raised off the bed. We all stared in disbelief. Chills ran throughout my whole body. Then plop—back on the bed he went. My sister Eva sobbed; Amy and I looked at each other in knowing. Robert was like, "Now that was the Holy Spirit." Everyone else looked on in disbelief.

I knew in my heart of hearts that the angels came to take my dad with his family right there in the room, and Dad said, "*No*, not yet!"

Eventually everyone else had left to go home, but I stayed. I just couldn't leave. Something kept telling me to stay. The priest that had baptized Dad less than a year earlier came after everyone had left. He was there to give Dad his last rites. I had never witnessed anyone receiving their last rites before. I was saying the parts for my dad—his last prayer before he left this world to go to heaven.

The priest was saying the prayer. I was right down by Dad's ear to make sure he could hear his last rites. I acted as if he were saying the prayer along with the priest. As we said the prayer, Dad started to moan and mumble throughout the prayer. The priest tried to ask him what he wanted; neither one of us could understand him. After the prayer, I leaned over and told my father, "It's all right if you want to go home; we will take care of Mom." Right after I said that, Dad took in a deep breath and let out a sigh. To me, that meant okay, thank you. Shortly after the priest left, I gave my father a kiss on the forehead; that was the last time I saw him alive.

It was only two hours later that I got the call from the hospital. Dad had passed away shortly after I left the room. I cried briefly and pulled myself together to call Mom. There was no more to do tonight. I felt sadness, emptiness, and relief. Dad wasn't suffering anymore. After all that happened in the hospital, I knew he joined the rest of his family in heaven. I knew from the fact that he was baptized and forgiven his sins a year earlier, and I knew from the angels who tried to take him in the hospital room with our family there as witnesses. Peace be with you, Dad!

Undeniable

We are born, and that in itself is a miracle.
We are a gift, each of us. One to the other.
He plans our path long before we arrive.

One has blue eyes, one has brown, the other green eyes.
Our skin does not matter, not to Him; He loves us equally.
This is a test for you and me, who will pass and who will fail.

It is undeniable these gifts in disguise.
A loved one, so young and innocent, suffers tremendous pain.
Then taken away—it's just another test, one of life's lessons.

What will we learn? How will we grow? Can we teach these lessons?
These are all lessons of love and loss. Can we do the job we were sent here
to do?
It is all just a test for you and me. Will you pass and walk the path you
were chosen for?
It is undeniable. We are all here for the same reason: to love, to teach, to
grow.

CHAPTER 15

September 2007: Bipolar 1

If you live in denial, whatever it is that you are denying, it will return to you tenfold.

I was rolling along, maybe not so merrily, but I was getting by the best I knew how. It had been fourteen months since my first manic episode. Nothing in my life had changed, except I had to see a psychologist every three months in order to get my bipolar medications. I was compliant with taking my medications when I wanted to.

I had ignored the doctor's diagnosis. I was in no way going to let them label me with a mental illness. I knew that the stress in my life was what had caused my breakdown. There was no way anyone could convince me otherwise.

The longer I got away without taking my medications, the more I knew I didn't have this "bipolar." So, I started out slow, with just forgetting occasionally to take my medication, and then it was like I was challenging myself to see if I would notice a difference when I didn't take my meds for three or four days.

The funny thing I have learned over the years is that bipolar is not predicable at all. You can feel really good one day, and then bam! There it is—you're out of control. Not sleeping, getting hyper, and acting irrational. Oh, if we could just tell when to stop!

My first memory of not acting quite right was the day I called my mother-in-law, Sharon. I used to avoid going to see most of my husband's family as much as I could. I felt insecure enough with myself; I didn't need any help from them to have a reason to hate myself. I did a great job at that all by myself for years.

I called Sharon to see if she would like to hear a CD by Nora Jones. I had just fallen in love with her songs and her style of composing; I knew Sharon would appreciate her sound. She said, "Yes; come on down." She lived down back from us, so I walked in my bare feet, which I would never have done if I was in my right mind. I have extremely sensitive feet. I have bone spurs and corns. So, I would have been in extreme agony from the dirt and rocks.

After Sharon and I had listened to the CD and talked as if we were old friends, I headed home. On my way home, I noticed a triangle-shaped clearing in the sky. I was mesmerized by this awesome sign. To me, it was the three points of the Catholic Church, the Trinity. Meaning the top was the Father, the right side was the Son, and the left side was the Holy Spirit. I remember stopping and sitting on the bench that was on the lawn and just reveling in how close I felt to God at that very moment.

After I was full of the Holy Ghost, so to speak, I came home. I started cleaning out my work van. Literally cleaning it out. I was tired of working and tired of not spending time with my kids and tired of my husband's drinking and cheating. I was done.

My manic episode was going into overdrive. As I threw things out of my van, my mind was racing with thoughts of cleaning up my life. Being in control by clearing out the clutter and the work. I remember throwing the keys to my van in the woods.

Before I went into the house, I saw the white porcelain girl and boy that sat on a bench. I bought this when we first moved in to the house. I thought it represented William and me and our love. Well, I stopped short and threw the porcelain figurines and the bench as far as I could. The boy's head came rolling off. I felt great! "There, you son of a bitch." I realize now that my anger was coming out toward William and his drinking and cheating and how he treated our children.

When I went into the house, Ann Marie was home, just getting up and getting ready for her day. She was listening to her music, which I believe was her saving grace living in such utter chaos.

So, I went to my master bathroom and bedroom, and I was frantically thinking. Thinking, thinking. Clean, clean, clean. Pure, pure, pure. I ripped the whole shower curtain down out of the shower. I didn't mess around with taking the hooks off one at a time. I ripped that sucker right down. I laid the shower curtain down on the carpet in the bedroom. I got the shampoo, the soap, the toothpaste, deodorant—I got anything that represented cleanliness out of the bathroom. I got things out of the bedroom that I felt represented love, and I put them on the bed. I got a nightie out of my drawer, pictures and jewelry. I put our wedding rings on the bed; they were the ultimate symbol of our love.

In the computer room, where all of William's online cheating started many years ago, I put anything dirty by the computer. Anything that reminded me of cheating and was dirty. There was a picture of one woman from Florida. She was William's "friend"; I found her number in his cell phone, and I called her. I needed to find out who she was and what her number was doing in his phone. When she realized it was me, she hung up as quickly as she could. William told me he talks to her online and on his cell phone. She has a husband that is bipolar, and they just talk. What I wanted to know was why she was wearing a bikini top and lying out like she was in heat in the photo that I found of her in his lunch box.

In my search for things to put on the computer desk, I walked by a picture of my daughter, Ann Marie. For years everyone has told me she is my favorite, that I treat her better than my boys. Well, a fleeting thought of letting her go flashed through my mind. I would show them that I didn't feel she was better than my boys and I could let her go. I threw her picture down the stairs. I forgot that the frame had glass in it, and I also forgot Ann Marie was downstairs. Almost immediately after I threw the picture down the stairs, she came running out of her room to see what happened. She said with anger and annoyance in her voice, "Mom? What are you doing?" I said, "Nothing," and she said, "Look what you did." I just shrugged my shoulders, turned around, and went back to the master bedroom.

While I continued to "clean" the bedroom, I put stuff on the shower curtain on the floor. I put items that meant love on the bed. Ann Marie had called her dad to tell him something was wrong with me.

William showed up from work, and I was running to get away from him. I was throwing things out the bedroom window. I was hollering, and I was totally letting him know that what had been going on for the past seven years was not okay. When I look back on everything that had unfolded to that point with my manic episode, I wonder, if I was able to get pissed off and face William with his cheating and drinking before I had stopped taking my pills, would I have gone into a manic episode? I question myself and my mental illness! If I had learned as a child how to handle pain and stress and fear and loss, would my "mental" illness have been diagnosed?

Well, William had called some friends of ours, Mark and Cindy. He thought they might be able to convince me to go to the hospital. I remember running around to avoid William. He was the bad guy. Mark, our friend, was the sweetest guy you could ever meet. He eventually talked me into getting into his truck. He then somehow talked me into going to the hospital with William.

It was just getting good as William and I took off in my van. He found the keys in the woods of course. They were looking for like twenty minutes before I almost busted a gut laughing at them.

So, William and I headed to town to go to the mental hospital. As William was driving, I was talking out of my head a mile a minute. I got it into my head to play this game. I would open the car door and pretend I was going to jump out of the van. I did that several times. I could see the fear in his eyes, and I just laughed. I wanted him to suffer somehow. He pleaded with me to stop. He pleaded with me to lie back and just rest. If that made him a little nervous, good, it was worth it for all he had put me through. I now question my actions with the game of trying to jump out of the car. How far would I have gone? Would I have really jumped? I could have been hurt or even killed.

So, we arrived at the mental hospital, and they refused to take me in. I had to go to our local hospital for processing and evaluation. So, we checked in at the hospital, got processed, and then I got my $350.00 ride back to the mental hospital after my evaluation via ambulance.

When I arrived at the mental hospital, I then get processed. There were testing and questions and paperwork to fill out. They took all of my belongings—my rings, watch, jewelry, and pocketbook. I was then led to the lockdown area.

After a few days on medication, I was a little more alert. On one of my first nights at the hospital, I saw a patient that had been admitted. He had on white pants and a white shirt; he had white bandages covered in blood wrapped around his head. He had a long beard and mustache. My first thoughts were, *that was Jesus.* Even though I thought it was Jesus, I feared him. They put this guy in a special room. The only thing he had was a mattress on the floor. Nothing else. He was a high-risk patient.

This guy screamed all night long. One time I was walking the halls at night because that's what I did when I couldn't sleep. This guy was in the hallway on the floor, screaming and fighting like five staff people. They of course would give him a shot, and he would go to sleep.

That night—I don't know why, but I was uneasy and couldn't sleep. I walked the hallways, looking for something, someone. I heard that guy screaming. I walked and walked, and I eventually came to my destination. I came to a window by the end of the hall. I had my hands raised up, as if to accept Jesus Christ. I saw in the window, whether on the inside or the outside, I was not sure. There stood Jesus Christ. I kissed the windowpane; it was Jesus's feet. I then went back down the hall to my room. The whole time I walked down the hall, I was aware of the staff watching me, but I didn't care. I was just drawn down the hallway to meet Jesus and kiss his feet.

With this manic episode, I saw all religious figures and people; my journey during my manic episode this time was like walking the Stations of the Cross. I felt like God was with me the whole time, giving me guidance and love through this whole process.

Little did I know that each time I was having a manic episode, I was learning more about myself. Fear, hate, and the things that I really wanted were surfacing. I now had to face the bipolar I and figure what it truly was and how I could get control of it.

Denial

To deny yourself of the things that are meant to be
Is like cutting off your air supply from your lungs.
When you hold your breath, you will eventually need to breathe.
When you deny the fate of your journey, the journey that God
Has set up for you, it will come the easy way or the hard way.
Denial can only slow the process. Keeping you from learning.
Keeping you from your destiny.

CHAPTER 16

God and Me

I have had a "knowing" of God for many years. My earliest memories of God were when I was three years old. I remember attending our local Baptist Church. I remember the ringing of the bell to let everyone know church was about to begin.

The thing I remember most about the church was Jesus's picture up front. I didn't know much about Him other than his eyes would constantly draw me into His picture. I remember everything was white and blue and gold at the church. The pews were your normal hardwood uncomfortable pews, but the rest was beautiful. I remember the singing, and I would get to see other kids that I knew.

Mom and Dad didn't take us to church. It was our neighbors down the road. I remember the girl because I ended up going to school with her later. I was told the reason why Mom and Dad didn't take us to church, and I am sure it was true. The Clayborn family picked us up to take us to church so Mom and Dad could have a little bit of Sunday all to themselves. My sister's words were "to get rid of us for a while on Sunday."

I remember at Christmastime, we had a play. It was a Christmas play, and all the children were so happy and excited to take part in this event. I remember after the play there were gifts for everyone. I remember getting a bag of salted popcorn with candy in it. I was very excited. So, my experience with God and everything associated with Him was good right from the beginning.

As I got older, I moved from the Baptist Church to the Pentecostal Church. I was about six years old, and I remember receiving gifts for coming to church the first time. If you got someone else to come, you would then receive another prize from the little wooden chest up front. I tried really hard to get other people to come. I so wanted to get a new toy every week. This was the church where I saw my first baptism. They had a huge tub of water, and they would bend the person who was getting baptized over this huge tub and put his or her head in water and talk really fast. I was quite scared of this process. I never wanted anyone to hold my head underwater.

There were a couple other churches somewhere after the Pentecostal Church. In my teens I was introduced to the Catholic Church. I was introduced to St. Paul's church by Elaina. She was a woman that would I babysit for throughout my teen years. She became my God mother when I was baptized in the Catholic Church. I got a lot of peace from going to the Catholic Church.

I knew there must be a more peaceful way of living than the hell that I had been enduring mentally and physically and the sexual abuse. It seemed like it was just way too much for such a young person to endure.

When I was fifteen years old, Elaina offered to take me to a swearing-in ceremony for a new nun. I was so excited. Not just to get away from my horrible homelife, but also to witness someone vowing to be faithful to Jesus for the rest of her life.

I was in awe of the whole experience. I loved the feeling of peace and love that everyone emanated. The ceremony was absolutely beautiful, and this girl was so young and she knew exactly what she wanted. I envied her. I envied the peacefulness that she had and the love that she felt so strongly about, and I wanted that for myself.

I met a nun while I was there. Her name was Sister Margaret. Sister Margaret and I wrote back and forth for a few years, and then I just stopped. I'm not sure what changed. I do remember wanting that peaceful serene type of life for myself. I knew deep in my heart that I wanted children more than I would have wanted to be one with God. So that dream of becoming a nun was replaced with my wanting to have children and to get married.

I was an active member of the Catholic Church right through my children's teens. We didn't go all the time, but I still considered myself active. I met Charles and Cindy, and we were very close friends; they were Latter-Day Saints, and I attended their church on and off over a four-year period. Then I attended a very active well-known Pentecostal Church a few towns over. I was baptized there. I was just beginning to enter my manic episode of 2007 at this point.

I have felt an urge to have Jesus Christ in my life from an early age, and when I am at my most stressful stages in my life, I feel Him tugging and pulling me back in. I feel He is with me the most when I'm with my bipolar. I didn't realize it until after my dad's death and my manic episode in 2007. If you allow Him to be part of your life and help you through whatever situation you're going through, He will be there.

Faith's Struggle

They say Jesus loves me …

This I did not know.

God and me, it is like a tug-of-war,

A battle throughout the years.

I know His strength is great and His love even greater.

How do you continue to believe when there is so much pain everywhere?

He gives us good. He gives us life. He gives us precious gifts.

Without warning He takes it all in one breath.

Gone forever.

I turn away. I want to run from You.

How could You?

Take, Take, Take.

It hurts so deep, I fear I will drown.

The tears will not come. How could You hurt me, hurt the ones I love?

I believe and have faith in You even though there is so much pain.

So much sorrow, but I return time and time again.

Because my faith in Your love brings me back.

To me, to self-love, to finding me!

Chelsey

CHAPTER 17

May 2014: The Vivid Dream

I was dreaming in my dream. I woke up in my dream, and I was surrounded by spirits. It was dark, and there were shadows all around me. I could not make out any faces. It was like they were floating back and forth slowly. I was back in my childhood home. My old bedroom. When I woke up in my dream, I saw and felt the many spirits in my room. I felt a little scared. I felt a hand on my left shoulder. I did not look back to see, but it was my dad. How I knew, I do not know. I just knew it was him. A feeling of calmness came over me at that moment.

There were other spirits in the room besides my father. I could only make out a few of them. I knew one spirit to be Chelsey. Chelsey was my best friend Carol's daughter. Chelsey and her boyfriend had gotten hit by a cement truck while backing out of a driveway almost ten years earlier. They both lost their lives that day. I saw my grandparents and a few aunts who were there. The room was overflowing with spirits. It's not as if I could see their faces to recognize them; I just knew. It's a feeling: when you know, you just know. Kind of like we have never seen God, yet we just know that He does exist.

After communicating with one of the spirits, a spirit entered into my body. I moved in a wavelike motion, and I felt the spirit come into my body. I felt that sensation in the here-and-now dream.

In my dream I felt a little uneasy about what had just happened. I got out of bed and went into the hallway. My cell phone began to ring in my dream. The ringing noise had static. It was like something was interfering with its connection. I answered the phone with a question in my voice. "Jesus?" I said. I paused, and there was no answer. I thought that was weird, and I hung up the phone.

I went down the hallway by the dining room where Mom's buffet was, and there was this light coming out of the top of my head. I tried to look up to see this light. When I moved, the light moved. The light was still shining, like a huge beacon out of the top of my head. I tried to feel it, and I could not feel hot or cold coming out of it. It was just a light.

I went to Mom and Dad's room. They were sleeping. I tried to wake up my mother. I gently shook her and whispered, "Mommy, Mamma, Mommy, Momma," like the baby from a popular adult cartoon. She did not stir or wake up.

I woke up from this vivid dream and felt odd. I knew this dream had a tremendous significance. I knew I needed an answer. I knew they had websites and books on what dreams mean. I chose to see a Reiki master. I needed someone I could trust to help me figure out what this dream meant.

I had been seeing a chiropractor for neck and back pain. I found out after just a few visits that he was a wonderful down–to-earth man. As we talked and got to know each other, he suggested his Reiki master. I went to see

Sheila, who had her master's 3 in Reiki. A few weeks after this dream occurred, I set up an appointment with her.

In my Reiki session, Sheila and I had a conversation. I told her a little about myself, and I told her about my dream. She told me she had never had anyone that had experienced such an intense dream before. Sheila told me what I could expect from her Reiki session.

Sheila instructed me to get on the table for my Reiki session. I got up on the table for her Reiki healing part of the session. I lay on my back, and I had my hands down to my sides. I tried to relax, and I took deep breaths in through the nose and out through the mouth. My eyes were closed, and I felt the warmth from her hands as they went from one chakra point to another. While she moved from one chakra point to another, she did not touch me. Reiki is done with energies from one body to the other. I felt many sensations as she passed over each chakra system.

Just as she was finishing up, she asked me, "Who is John?" I thought of John, a young man who had been very helpful to me while I lived in my trailer. She said, "No, this one is not living." It took me a few minutes, as I remember. Then it hit me right between the eyes! She was talking about my best friend Carol; she had a son who was John. Chelsey, my best friend Carol's daughter, was trying to get through to me. She was sending me a message from the other side. Sheila said, "Do you need more information?" I started to cry, and my back was in horrible pain. As I was crying, I told Sheila, "No; I know what Chelsey wants."

Chelsey came to me in a Reiki session. She wanted me to give her mom a message—to stop driving John crazy. John was going for his driver's license, and Chelsey wanted Carol to know that she was watching over John and he would be fine.

Sheila was floored. She has never had someone in Spirit come through in a Reiki session, she told me at the end of the session, giving light to everything that had transpired during the session and my dream. She thought that it would be best to see her spiritual shaman. She thought that I was over her head and that I needed someone with more knowledge than what she was able to help me with.

I felt so many emotions after this session. I felt honored that Chelsey came to me through my Reiki session. I wondered why she didn't come through when I was at a psychic medium show earlier that summer. I felt nervous. How would Carol feel? She had been wanting Chelsey to come through, to talk to her for so long, and now, I ended up giving her this kind of lighthearted message.

It was a couple of days before I was able to get to Carol's. I knew I couldn't call her, or she would be suspicious of why I wanted to see her. Even though we are best friends, we go months and months and as much as a year without seeing each other. On a Friday night, I drove an hour from my house to see Carol. I was praying the whole way there that she would be home.

I finally got there, and there was only one vehicle in the driveway, no lights, and it was kind of late for a visit. It was after seven o'clock. I got out of my car, went to the door, and knocked. Carol couldn't believe I was there. Carol, no matter how much shit life throws at her and there has been a lot, she always has this infectious laugh, and her smile is the most beautiful thing I have ever seen. Carol practically yelled, "Oh, my God, what are you doing here?" I of course played it cool. "Oh, just needed to see you." She knew different.

We went into her bedroom after saying my hellos to Matt, her husband. John was out with his friend and would be home later.

So Carol and I sat in her room on her bed. She said, "Well, what? Tell me, tell me why you're here." I just started to cry. Then she started to cry. Through tears and trying to talk while being all emotional, I said, "Chelsey came to me." Carol said, "What?" I told her about the Reiki session and how Chelsey wanted me to tell her to stop driving John crazy, that she was watching over him and he would be okay driving.

Carol said to me in the calmest voice ever, "I know she is watching over John." Carol and I had the longest conversation in history that night. She and I can go years without seeing one another, and it would be just like we talked yesterday. I cherish our friendship, and I thank God for putting her into my life. There are certain people God puts in our lives, and they are pure gifts from heaven. Throughout my life with my family, working as a CNA and direct support worker, and running my own business, I have met some of the most beautiful people and have learned and been taught many lessons.

I have had many dreams in my lifetime. Some were good, and some were pure nightmares. This dream that I had that led to a Spirit encounter was indeed a precious gift. Pay attention to your dreams, for they may very well be a gift for you.

Dreaming of You

I see colors and darkness all around me.

There is a fog that is within my head.

I cannot tell if I am awake or dreaming.

I feel calmness, yet there is this fear that I cannot explain.

I am surrounded, by whom, I know not.

A message, I fear, is coming from You.

Will I understand it? Will I be strong enough to do the things You need done?

I see the light, the light of the One. Your message is clear.

Your will be done!

You sent her to me. It was so unexpected; if I had only been prepared.

If I only knew how to accept your gift.

The signs are getting clearer; your work of love will not go undone.

I will pass on the messages that you send me,

One at a time!

Dreaming of You will bring me the peace that I need to help myself and those that I love!

Dreaming of You!

Bella Louise

CHAPTER 18

May 2014: Bipolar 1 and PTSD

The primary diagnosis for my third stay at the mental hospital was bipolar I and Post Traumatic Stress Disorder. The events leading to my hospitalization this time were recent discontinuation of medications, increased manic symptoms, and psychosis. I was hospitalized from May 19, 2014, to May 27, 2014.

The one thing that differed for me with this hospitalization versus my other two stays was that I asked for help. I knew I was in the middle of a manic episode and needed help. I had never before been coherent enough to know that I needed intervention to get help. I ask myself, *why? Why did I catch myself this time?*

I remember the struggle to keep my wits about me. I felt the fear. I had been aware that I wasn't quite right for over two weeks. So, how did I not just lose it like the other two times?

Let me share with you the things over the past two years that had happened and I still hung on to my sanity. I stayed stable even without using my lithium for my brain imbalance and my Depakote for my mood stabilizer.

In March 2012, I went in for my gastric bypass surgery, which I was looking forward to. I finally could see the light at the end of the tunnel with my weight issues. I weighed 356 pounds at my heaviest, and I was having so many health issues. I had fluid retention throughout my body. I had fluid on my lungs, which made my Chronic Obstructive Pulmonary Disease worse. My smoking two packs of cigarettes a day didn't help. My sciatic nerve made it difficult to walk and get around. It interfered with my work, not to mention my ability to try to lose weight. Who wants to walk to lose weight when the nerve in your ass going down the back of your leg is in excruciating pain?

The day I walked the short distance to my mailbox and had chest pains and pains down my left arm, I knew I had to do something. I needed more help than I could give myself. I ended up calling the surgical weight loss program at our local hospital.

I went to all of the required classes and did all the prep work to have the surgery. I didn't have an easy time with the surgery, however. After my first surgery, I had an abdominal leak and had to go in for another surgery to repair the leakage. Five days later I ended up back under the knife because I had five blockages that needed to be repaired. After three surgeries and almost dying after the second surgery and knowing I met my friend Charles on the other side, I had to make the decision whether I would stay here on earth or go to the other side, to heaven. I chose coming back because I sit here now and I write the book I was supposed to write nine years ago.

After my three major stomach surgeries, I had nothing but trouble with trying to eat and especially getting my pills down. I remember gagging and vomiting my pills time and time again. So, yet again I became noncompliant with taking my medications that I needed to keep me stable mentally and out of the hospital.

I went through three job changes trying to find my niche in the workplace. Where did I fit in? Where was I comfortable doing what I loved the most? Where could I work full-time and still squeeze in some housekeeping every now and then? Well, I finally found the job match for me, and it was of course taking care of mentally and physically challenged adults. I love my clients and will probably be here for quite a while.

So, I was happy at my new job, and just a week into the new job, my dad was hospitalized. Dad was not well at all this time. This would be the last time Dad went into the hospital. The doctors explained to us that the dialysis that Dad was receiving was no longer effective and it was not taking care of the fluid in his body. The doctors also told us that he had an infection in his blood. Dad was going sepsis. It was only a matter of time, and we needed to make the decision to continue with dialysis or take him off and let him go peacefully.

I was still dealing with not being compliant with my medications and losing my dad. I had changed jobs, and then I was moving, and my children were extremely upset with me for telling them I was selling my trailer. There was so much stress and drama going on. I don't know how I stayed strong enough to get through this without a manic episode.

I have learned a lot about myself over the past few years, and I can be strong through the worst situations; but it's when things slow down and are calm, that's when everything hits me. It settles in and knocks me for a loop.

As I put one foot in front of the other in my day-to-day life, I search still for my purpose and reason for being here. We all have a reason. Between counseling, my religion, raising my children, and the Reiki that I was trying to bring back in my life, I looked desperately for answers, life's purpose. Is there really more to this life than what we see?

I saw a psychic medium just before my last manic episode. It was an awesome sight to see someone who was at peace and full of love trying to help these poor people. People who were looking to keep their faith alive. Hoping to hear a message from their loved ones. People who just wanted a chance to see that we can still have contact and a relationship with our loved ones that have crossed over. I wanted so bad to have my sister Eva get a reading while at the show. It wasn't meant to be. I, however, got to get a signed copy of the medium's book, and I bought her two CDs to help learn how to communicate and open the portal to connect with my loved ones who have crossed over.

Between this psychic's show and her CDs to help with communicating with our loved ones, I then started doing Reiki on myself. I was opening up my chakra system and my portal to my loved ones who had moved on.

I had my vivid dream, and things started to happen. I still believe these things truly were happening to me. I just didn't know how to slow things down. I was hearing subliminal messages from the TV and the radio. When I looked at street signs or some license plates, they all had some significance to me. I saw a license plate with death 13. My father died in 2013. I saw one that had my best friend's name: Carol-75. I have seen this license plate again within the past month.

I had some of the abilities that a psychic would have. I was able to hear and feel spirits around me. The weirdest thing that happened for me during this time was when I went to our local shopping center. I kept hearing voices. I was hearing voices of all the children. Children that had passed on. They were all talking at the same time. At first I thought it was just me hearing things. Then this one guy I heard, he kept hollering, "John, John." It felt like the closer I got to the front of the store, it was louder and louder. It was such an intense feeling, overwhelming to say the least. Was I really experiencing this spirit coming through, or was I losing it again?

There was a guy that I saw while in the store, and it seemed like he was following me in the store that morning. This guy was then at the next store that I went to. I got really uncomfortable when I got in my car to leave after getting groceries at my third stop that morning. Boom, there he was again, and he stared at me while he walked by. I felt scared. I wasn't sure if he was good spirit looking for me to pass on a message or if he was a bad spirit working on my mental state.

When I got into my car, I was so overwhelmed with all that had transpired that morning, I just sat in my car for a minute. Trying to calm myself down. My cell phone rang and scared the shit out of me. My sister Amy was calling. In the past few weeks, it was like I was on this wavelength with the people I needed the most, and she must have felt I needed help.

I told her all that had happened, and she told me I needed to get to the emergency room. So I told her I would.

As bad as I was falling apart, I held it together. I called my boyfriend's mom. I asked her if she could give me a ride to the emergency room because I needed to get evaluated. She said yes, she could do that.

I never struggled so hard in my entire life to stay mentally together. My body was one tense strand from head to toe. I was picturing myself losing it, hallucinating and driving off the road, killing myself, hurting someone else. It was the longest ride of my life. I drove myself to my boyfriend's mom's house.

I stayed together throughout this whole process. It seemed like it took me forever to arrive at Grace's. I knew what needed to be done to keep the business going, and my boss needed to be called. I had everything taken care of for my cleaning business and for my personal care job. I knew I would be spending yet again another week or more back at the mental hospital.

I felt disappointment in myself, failure as a person trying to get through life. I feared letting my boyfriend Seth down. I was embarrassed that his family would judge me for being crazy. I am always worried that everyone thinks I'm crazy. I remind myself almost daily that I am not crazy. I am strong. I am worth love, and I deserve to have everything I want.

So, my stay at the hospital was for eight days. I don't remember being so drugged up this time. I remember meeting a girl there, and guess what! She was a Reiki master. She knew how to ground me and helped me to remember to breathe, and she even worked her magic on an out–of-control patient. The doctors and nurses allowed her to do it as long as she did not touch anyone. Reiki is healing, using good energy from one person and mentally giving this good energy to another person. The doctors were amazed with the work she did.

I ran into a friend at the hospital this time. I felt lucky that I was in a different state of mind this time. It's amazing what you learn when your eyes are open and your heart has a knowing that the doctors still are not able to wrap their heads around. I would watch the people around me. The counselors would ask questions, and every now and then I would answer them. I knew to keep my answers to what modern medicine would expect a "normal" person to respond with.

I have learned that yes, there is more out there than what the human can comprehend. I feel that I am not ready for the spirits to have me passing on their messages. One of the few gifts that I do still use today is when I pass by a penny on the ground. I pick it up, and I check the date. The date is a message from a loved one. Sometimes it is a date that is significant to you or someone you know. I have found several pennies with meaning to me.

I found a penny under my mother's rug in her bedroom. It had the date 1985. That was her twenty-fifth wedding anniversary year. I found this penny just a couple of days before Mom's birthday. To me that was her gift from Dad. I found one penny that was dated 1901. That was my favorite grandmother's birth year. A single white feather on the ground is a kiss from a loved one. The time 11:11 on the clock is a wink from a loved one in heaven. I see this one almost every day, twice a day. My father's spirit is a dragonfly. The sign for my best friend's daughter is a rainbow. Her Indian name means rainbow as well. My favorite is when I see a double rainbow. That is significant to her and her boyfriend, who passed together.

We are all able to see the signs from our loved ones. We just have to believe and have faith, and the signs will come and you too will have a knowing of what is your sign from your loved one. I use the little gifts that I have and know that someday I will be ready to pass on the messages that are meant to be sent on—just not today.

Acceptance of Me

It seems like forever since I have seen you.

You were just a girl.

Blonde hair and blue eyes.

You didn't have a care in the world.

Where did you go?

I have missed you so.

Your bright smile could fill a room.

You were so small,

And then you were gone.

You have grown so much through the years.

So much abuse, so much sadness.

No wonder you were lost,

Lost within yourself.

How did you survive?

All the pain and fear kept you from you.

After all these years, you still give,

Give of you.

You never ask for anything in return.

With all of His lessons, the hardest one has been

Acceptance, acceptance of you.

Sam, Stephen,& Ann Marie

CHAPTER 19

Our Little Miracle

Miracles happen every day. Most of us never learn to appreciate the miracles that God sets before us. In all the experiences in my lifetime, there has never been a miracle of such utter and complete joy as that of the birth of my grandson. Stephen James Allen Tyler was born on November 20, 2014, at 10:56 p.m.

Stephen decided he would arrive three weeks early. My daughter Ann Marie had started to have the Braxton Hicks contractions on November 19. It was no big deal. Every woman can have the Braxton Hicks. It is a natural part of a woman's body getting ready for the birth process. The next morning, however, Ann Marie was experiencing contractions. She didn't want to panic, so she got ready and went to work; she did her normal routine at work.

I called Ann Marie at work around ten thirty to see how she was doing, and she calmly told me she was waiting for a call back from the doctor's office. She told me she had started her contractions that morning at five thirty. When I called her back thirty minutes later, her contractions were ten to fifteen minutes apart. Ann Marie's doctor's office called her and wanted her to go to his office to get checked out.

I was working and had to get coverage so that I could be there for my baby girl. After my coverage was all set, I met Ann Marie at the doctor's office. She was set up on the baby monitor, and the contraction paper feed was reading her contractions. She was definitely having contractions. We now just had to wait for the doctor to check her cervix to make sure the contractions were going to advance and that this was not false labor.

By the time the doctor checked her cervix, she was dilated 2 to 2 1/2 centimeters, and her contractions were four to eight minutes apart. Ann Marie's cervix was thinning, and the doctor decided it was time for her to go to the hospital. Ann Marie was told it was okay to go to her house and shower and pack for the hospital. This of course was driving me insane. I thought it would be better to just get to the hospital in case things progressed along quicker than we anticipated. But she was calm and cool and was just taking her time to get things together.

We finally arrived at the hospital around three o'clock. We went straight to the delivery floor, and they got Ann Marie all prepped and set up for monitoring her and the baby. I could tell she was excited and nervous at the same time. The nurse suggested that she go for walks and told us that it would help the labor process move along a little quicker.

Ann Marie's contractions were getting stronger and closer together. She would breathe in through the nose and out through the mouth. As the labor pains got stronger and closer together, the doctor came in to check her cervix; and by five o'clock she was 50 percent effaced and 5 centimeters dilated. It was decided that our little miracle baby would soon be here to meet us.

As Ann Marie was in labor, Stephen never once settled down. It was like he was fighting to get out. It was like he had a purpose, and if he didn't come out soon, it wouldn't happen.

As time drew near, it got harder for Ann Marie to concentrate and breathe through her contractions.

Ann Marie's dad had come to help her through this. He coached her with her breathing and coached her to let her know she could do this. Grampy Allen held her hand and talked her through the pain.

Ann Marie was pushing with all of her might to get Stephen into this world. I could see the baby's head crowning; there was all of this beautiful black hair. At one point as his head was just peeking out, the doctor took his finger and ran it up and down the baby's head. It was as if he was trying to stimulate Stephen to the outside world. After what seemed like a lifetime, Stephen had stalled out and was stuck. All of a sudden, "Whoosh"—out flew our little miracle baby. The doctor was covered in amniotic fluid, and so was I. I was standing just a few inches from the doctor. The doctor caught him like he was a football. If the doctor hadn't jumped back, he probably would have missed.

Everything went really quick after that. I cut the baby's cord, and then they set Stephen on Ann Marie's chest just for a quick minute. Ann Marie and I exchanged concerned glances, but we said nothing. The nurses whisked him over to the babies' warming crib to check him out.

Stephen wasn't crying the way he should. He could only make crackling noises. Every mother's first joy after her baby is born is to hear the baby cry and wail. There were only little crackles coming out of our little miracle baby. His airway was compromised. But why we didn't know.

Never before had I felt this sinking feeling in my stomach. I stayed strong and positive for Ann Marie. She needed to know that if Mom was strong, maybe then she would be strong, and Stephen would be okay.

Stephen's first Apgar score was 8. That quickly changed because of his color and his inability to cry and take full breaths; it went down to 5. This was concerning, and the nurses whisks him to the NICU to get him checked out and to stabilize his airway.

I did get a few pictures of Stephen and Ann Marie and then one of Stephen with the nurse while she was checking him out. He was absolutely the most gorgeous little baby boy, and he had already stolen Meme's (my) heart.

The doctor came back shortly after they took Stephen to the NICU and told us that they would keep him in the NICU until the ENT specialists came to check him the next day. All that we knew was that our little five-pound, nineteen-inch miracle baby boy, Stephen James Allen Tyler, was having trouble breathing. The doctors were keeping him on his belly to make it easier for him to breathe. They would monitor him closely throughout the night and let us know if anything changed.

Ann Marie and I got to see Stephen the next morning. He was so very beautiful and so tiny. The ENT specialist explained they would put a scope down his throat to try to find out what was causing him to struggle to breathe.

The doctor gave us two scenarios. One was that Stephen's jaw was very tiny, and his tongue was keeping him from breathing correctly. The other was he might have a soft esophagus that would require several surgeries to reconstruct.

Well, they were wrong on both of those scenarios. After putting a scope down Stephen's tiny little throat later that morning, they found a large fluid-filled cyst. There was no known cause for the cyst. It was explained to Ann Marie and me that he would be flying to the General Hospital within the next few hours. Stephen was too small, and he needed to be in a facility where they had the proper equipment for the procedure that they would have to do.

Things got crazy from that moment on. We wanted to make sure Ann Marie had everything she needed for the trip, and we weren't sure how long she would be gone. The adrenaline was pumping in all of us. The emotions that you want and need to express—well, there was no time. We just had to suck it up, pack, and go. Ann Marie and Stephen were in their first helicopter ride by three thirty that afternoon, November 21, 2014. Daddy, Sam was on his way by bus shortly after Ann Marie and the baby left.

When they arrived at General Hospital, Ann Marie kept me informed as much as she could. They met with the Pediatric ENT specialist. Stephen had a feeding tube that went in his nose and down to his belly so he could have nourishment. He was also put on a respirator to help him get the good air exchange he would need for all of his body. He was given morphine so he wouldn't work so hard to breathe, and they also gave him other medications for preventing infections and to keep him comfortable.

He looked so tiny and so vulnerable. Stephen was so strong and fought so hard. Ann Marie and I are so proud of the determination that he has shown since the day of his ultrasound before he was born. Stephen knew there was something wrong, and he fought every step of the way to be with his mom and dad.

We met with the specialist, and he explained the procedure they would perform to relieve the cyst in Stephen's throat. On November 26, 2014, he had part of the top of his cyst removed just above the top of his voice box. The doctor felt it was too tricky a surgery for Stephen being so tiny, and he did not want to compromise his ability to talk. The doctor drained the cyst and left the rest of it in place. The doctor did a tracheotomy to help keep a safe airway for Stephen until his cyst was gone. The doctor said on December 1 he would go back in to check to see if the cyst was filling back up; if so, he would drain the cyst again and inject a soap and chemical solution to help shrink the cyst over time.

On November 30, 2014, Ann Marie got to hold her baby for the first time. It had been ten long agonizing days. She pumped her breasts faithfully, to keep her mind occupied and to keep her spirits up. She so wanted to breast-feed her little "Peanut." He has many nicknames, but that one seems to stick the best. Ann Marie was very patient while she waited for him to get better. She watched the nurses and helped them every chance she could get. She wanted to care for him and take part in everything they were doing. She wanted to be prepared to take care of her little "Peanut" when she got to take him home.

Ann Marie held Stephen for two hours. I can only imagine how good it felt for Mommy to finally hold her baby boy. I was so proud of her for how strong she was through this whole thing.

On December 1, the doctor went back in to check on the cyst, and it had not refilled with fluid, but he did inject the cyst to shrink it over time.

As Ann Marie and I waited for Stephen to heal from surgery, we hoped and prayed for him to get stronger. I watched my baby girl turn into a woman. Never in a million years did we expect all this drama and stress from the birth of this little miracle baby. I know God has a plan for everything. I don't know how I would have handled this. To work so hard to overcome the challenges that Stephen has had. My heart goes out to all of those moms and dads who have had the most precious gift ever given to them and then had the child taken away.

By December 6, 2014, Stephen had proven time and time again how strong he is and just how determined he is to stay with us. On the way home from

General Hospital, Stephen was getting all prepped and was ready to fly out when the life flight attendant who was going to give him his pacifier noticed that he was not breathing. The attendant gently shook Stephen to try to jolt him to breathe again, and there was no response. He then proceeded to do a sternum stimulation. It worked, and things went crazy from there. They couldn't risk sending him home due to his apnea, and they wanted to get him stabilized. Stephen never made it off the helipad.

The worst part was Ann Marie was already on a bus on her way back home. Ann Marie got a call from a nurse at the hospital while she was on the bus. They were unable to send Stephen because he was having periods of apnea. My baby girl was on her way home, and her little tiny baby was not coming home.

I felt so helpless. There was nothing in the whole world that I could do at that moment when she called me from the bus. She was coming home, and her baby would stay three states away. Ann Marie told me she felt so guilty. "What if something happens, and I'm not there?" she wondered aloud.

It wasn't until the next day that Ann Marie got back on the bus. She and Sam got on the bus to be with their baby. I can only imagine how long the ride was or how agonizing the night must have been.

The doctor ran a lot of tests. He needed to know why all of a sudden this little boy started to have apnea. The doctor ordered blood work, he checked for an infection in his blood, they did a spinal tap to check for spinal meningitis, and they did X-rays. All the tests came back fine. Nothing could explain why Stephen stopped breathing. He had several more episodes of apnea over the next few days.

Ann Marie found out shortly after all this drama that Stephen would get mad and hold his breath. He would cry really hard and just hold his breath.

I'm not sure if that was the issue that day on the helicopter or not, but it was a scary experience for all.

The doctors monitored Stephen for a few more days, and he was then transported back home. He stayed at our local hospital until just a few days before Christmas. Stephen got his Christmas wish to Santa. He just wanted to be home with Mom and Dad.

Stephen went back to General Hospital for a recheck a few months later, and his cyst had reduced in size and was doing well. The doctor wanted to keep his tracheotomy in until at least August while the cyst continued to shrink and hopefully he would get much bigger.

Stephen is doing very well today, even though he isn't able to cry and make all the cooing and giggling noises that all the other six-month-old babies make. I can say, however, that his not having the sense of speech has awakened his other senses tremendously.

Ann Marie and Stephen have taken American Sign Language lessons, and she practices with him daily. When I watch him, he just takes in everything around him. When he was really little, he would recognize a voice, like Mom's or Dad's; if he didn't recognize a voice, it would make him jump or he would be a little afraid.

Stephen has an attention span like no other child I've seen. When he was one month old, he watched the Super Bowl in his hospital bed for forty-five minutes nonstop, flailing his arms and kicking his legs. He was so excited. He will sit on the couch and watch and kick and flail his arms while watching TV. He bounces around in his Johnny Jump Up and watches TV until he falls asleep. His mom does the elimination communication program with him, and he has been working on potty training. I must say he does a wonderful job with that ever since four months old.

Stephen has a way of knowing whenever I am at his house. His mother makes me stay in the kitchen because if I go near his bedroom or into the living room, he wakes up. He senses that I am there! I just happen to be a very fun Meme, and I can tell he and I are going to have lots of fun together.

Stephen is a true miracle to me. He is my hero. I know in my heart of hearts that he has a reason greater than most of us will be able to understand for being here on earth. I just thank God for giving this precious little boy to us, and I thank Stephen for fighting so hard to stay with us.

I look forward to all the wonders Stephen will be bestowing on all of us while he is here on this great big planet.

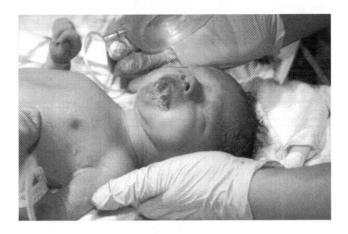

Meme's Hero

Definition—Hero: A person who is admired for great or brave acts or one who has fine qualities;

One who shows great courage;

An illustrious warrior.

On November 20, 2014, at 10:56 p.m., I finally met my hero, Stephen James Allen Tyler, five pounds, nineteen inches.

Stephen has shown Meme what it is to truly fight for life, and he has faced one struggle after another.

He has faced each struggle with a strength that is beyond words.

I love you, Stephen, for all your strength and determination to come into this world and your stubbornness not to give up. I know in my heart of hearts that your struggles are not to make you a stronger person, but to help those that watch you grow and love you, to make us stronger in faith and to love all that He has given us.

Meme loves you to infinity and beyond.

CHAPTER 20

April 2015: And the World Spins

As I try to write this book about my life, it could be crumbling around me. As I sit here writing to keep myself from falling apart, I wonder how long it will be before I give in to all of it. How do I stay strong and not let my own mental illness take over my racing brain? The fear will not stop.

I am at work trying to fill in for a friend who just had two heart attacks and flatlined. She shared with me her experience with dying; she was told it wasn't her time to go, and she had to go back. I worry for her because she is still not well. She has a long recovery ahead of her. I fear still for her life, and as I fear for her life, my son is just on the brink of a breakdown. He is threatening to shoot himself and says he doesn't want to live anymore.

I have been down this road before. The fear for his mental stability. The fear for his taking his own life. I sit here at work unable to leave, unable to check on him, unable to hold him, unable to make him want to live.

I work and take care of my clients; Department of Human Services is here, and I stay focused on my job. Billy's girlfriend is texting me and keeping my anxiety level up. My fear is still in full force, yet I stay calm through it all. Ten hours pass by since Courtney's first message. I have my clients in bed, and my work is all set.

I frantically tried to get hold of him all day. I called and sent text messages to his sister. Ann Marie tried to reach him, but there was no answer. I texted back and forth with his girlfriend Courtney. I called his father, who is out of state.

His father tried to call him and text him. No response. The last anyone heard from Billy was that he had reached his friend's house. As I worry and wonder, my anxiety rises to new heights.

It has been ten hours, and I fight with myself to call 911 or to call the 1-800 hotline. My fear for what everyone else will think of me for "overreacting" and being crazy overrides my knowledge of my son and his mental illness. The power of fear can overtake your whole sense of reality. The reality is that if I wait, it will be too late. They will find my baby boy with a gunshot wound to the head or dead from an overdose. My fear is that if I do call for help, he will never forgive me. If they take him back to the mental hospital, he will hate me forever. When do you listen to what you know to be true? My son has been in need of intervention for a long time.

Billy has a Facebook page like most of us do. As I follow his page and many others, I worry. First he's up with his posts, happy and excited that his life is going well, and then it's the total opposite of the spectrum. His Aunt Paulette talks to me; she has her worries and wonders what's going on with him. That gives me the knowledge that I am not the only one who is worrying about his state of mind. His brother Corey also says, "What the hell is going on with Billy?" With the added input of Corey worrying about Billy's attitude on Facebook, I feel better about being able to confront him and ask a few questions.

I saw Billy a few months ago, and I asked him how things were going. He said, "Fine." I asked him about his Facebook page and how depressed he seemed and said that I was worried. I told him if he needed anything, he just needed to come to me and ask. I reminded him about my mental illness and his. I told him that it can sneak up on you quickly, and it can be out of control before we know it. He told me he was good and not to worry. I told him it was my job to worry; I was his mother. As I always do, I told him I loved him. That is the one thing I have done since all of my babies were babies. "I love you," is always on our lips every day, no matter how angry we are at one another.

Billy was at work when he was supposed to be. His dad told me to go check on him if I was worried, and I told him I was at work and couldn't leave my clients. He then told me to call his work and just find out if he showed up. I did call, and he was working. Thank you, Jesus; at least the picture of him facedown-dead could stop. The car wrapped around a tree scenario could stop. He was at work, making money to pay his bills.

I didn't hear from Billy until the next day. At some point he sent me a private message through Facebook. He told me he was okay and that he was just stressed out.

Why would you threaten to shoot yourself and tell your girlfriend you didn't want to live another day? He said he did not remember saying it. He doesn't realize it, but there is a psychotic episode brewing; how bad it will get and what will happen, I do not know. I fear it and I feel it, but I push those feelings away; they are too painful to face, and it's too hard to try to convince anyone else that my fears are not "crazy"—they are real and right in my face. It is just a matter of time. Will Billy break first, or will I go manic?

Dizzy

The world around me spins, spins out of control.

I ask myself how do I stand tall and fight.

Everyone watches and judges me from their seats.

It is like a game—how long can I play before I lose?

Spinning, spinning, spinning faster,

How do I get off?

I fear everything I love will crumble and fall if I do not remain in control.

I must control my fear,

My thoughts,

My words, and my actions.

How do I control any of it, when it is all out of my control?

My babies mean the world to me, and I have done everything for them.

As I struggle to let them go, I fear for them.

Letting go.

No more control.

It is all in His hands.

Trust in Him.

If you do, your world will not spin.

It will slow down; it will be a calmer place to be.

No more fear.

Trust in Him, the One who has control.

Be dizzy no more!

CHAPTER 21

Finding Me

It's been a long hard road for me, but I am blessed in my life. I have many gifts from God.

Since my marriage of twenty-three years came to an end, my life has taken a positive turn. When I made the decision to ask for a divorce, it came easily. I knew my marriage had been in trouble for eight years or more. As the months and years went by and William and I grew further apart, it came down to one thing. I either waited until I faced another manic episode, or I could free myself from the anxiety-ridden marriage that was just existing. Our marriage was a piece of paper that had no meaning. Two lonely people swimming in a pool that would surely drown us both.

I of course had my usual anxiety as the day progressed. I knew it was way overdue to end my marriage. It was, however, a sad day when I passed my daughter's bedroom, and I overheard the conversation. Ann Marie and my youngest son Corey were having a conversation. All I can remember is Ann Marie saying, "I don't know why they don't just get a divorce; all they do is fight." I felt sad, sad that my children were smarter than me. I was the adult; I was trying to hold onto this marriage until my children were grown and gone. I feared being alone. I feared my children would not have a "normal family." Little did I know, we were far from a normal family, a normal healthy family. There was anxiety daily with myself and the kids. There was frustration on William's part. There was so much anger and so many tears. Too many tears from all of us. It wasn't just the bipolar that I had; it was my son Billy's illness, Corey's depression and anxiety, William's drinking and staying out all hours of the night. It all was just getting to be too much for me to handle. It was the whole dynamics of our family. We had all been in therapy at one time or another. Therapy was just never enough.

When you are in denial of the issues in front of you, they lie dormant and fester like a boil. When everyday life and pressures of work and school and mental illness come together without the proper medical attention, things will and do explode.

I decided to do the only thing I knew I could do. To save myself from going back to the hospital, I asked for a divorce. William was calm and said, "Whatever you want." I knew I wanted him to fight, even just a little. His answer told me everything. He had wanted a divorce but was afraid to ask. I let it go; I just wanted out. I wanted to feel whole again; I wanted the feelings of anxiety gone; I didn't want to cry anymore.

It wasn't long before I found a place. I moved out of the house that I had worked so hard for. On March 18, 2009, I found a rent-to-own trailer just three miles down the road. I was feeling very good about the move, and the divorce was coming along as well as a divorce can.

The trailer I found was perfect. It was a later model trailer, and it only had two owners. It was in great shape. It had a small deck on the front and a large deck with privacy lattice on the back. I had my own storage shed and a fire pit and a small vegetable garden. The kids could visit with their dad easily, and it was closer to town for the extensive traveling that I did with my business.

I found it hard to get used to a new routine. I'd always had the anxiety of wondering when William would get home or where he was or who he was with. It felt weird missing that feeling of anxiety, the ball in the pit of my stomach. It took two weeks for me to settle into a routine and decide, *hey, this isn't so bad.*

Ann Marie was away at college; Billy and Corey moved in with me, into the little trailer park with really close neighbors. It wasn't long before Billy and Corey ended up back in their routine of knock-down, drag-out fights. They brought one such fight outside for all in the trailer park to see. You want to see anxiety go from 0 to 60? It did that day for me. I was supposed to be starting a new life, and we brought the same behaviors that I struggled with daily to try to get under control, even to stop. The hate and the craziness.

It just about killed me when Corey came to me and said, "Mom, I'm going to move back with Dad." As much as I hated the thought of my baby not being with me, I knew from past experience that if Corey stayed, the fighting would continue. That would not be good for me or our very close neighbors.

The week of May 5, 2009, I had a barbeque. I have always loved entertaining and having family and friends over. This was my first time to actually have family over and not feel like I would have to play referee. There were at least twenty-five people that came to help celebrate the beginning of a new life for me and the beginning of summer and just to enjoy themselves.

That's the day when I finally met the "boy" next door. He was trying to put a grill on his back deck, and I offered to help him. I of course was nervous like no tomorrow. We finally met, talked, and broke the ice. His name was like butter coming off of my tongue—Seth. Seth and I would just by chance meet on our lawn every chance we got. First five minutes, then twenty minutes, and then we graduated to the front deck for conversation for hours on end. We were building a friendship like I had never had before. It was three months before we graduated to the next level. I had never enjoyed a man's company more than I did then and still do today. It has been six years, and God could not have put a more perfect match together. I thank my lucky stars every day for moving to the trailer park.

Seth and I became friends, then lovers. After we had been seeing each other for four years, Seth was making plans to build a house or to move, and I panicked. He didn't see it the same way. He was so excited the day he knew he found his house. He surprised me. Seth told me, "Pack your bags; you're coming with me." I was so happy and excited, I just wanted to cry. All my fears went out the door. In June 2013 Seth and I moved into a beautifully renovated home, and we have been here for two years now.

I work as a direct support worker, and I still do my cleaning business part-time. We have a very spoiled cat named Dexter, and we enjoy each other's company like I never thought possible. We don't fight; Seth told me he saw enough fighting in growing up, and that he wasn't a fighter, he is a lover. I love that about him.

My children are living their lives, struggling the struggle of life. I see them or contact them often. My daughter has blessed me with my first grandchild, Stephen James Allen Tyler. He is the love of my life. I see Stephen as often as I can. I help my children as much as I can, and I wish them all the best in their journey.

I feel content in my life with Seth, but I do still struggle daily with my bipolar. I am compliant with my medications. On my last psychiatry visit, I was told, "Bella, no matter how compliant you are with your medications, stressors in your life can send you reeling into a manic episode just as easily as being off of your medications." I have done my best with the lessons that I have learned while living with bipolar for the past thirteen years. It is an illness that has no cure. It can only be managed by the individual who suffers from it by staying compliant with your medications, seeking therapy, and the thing I struggle most with—managing my stress and getting plenty of sleep.

It is not easy in this world that we live in to limit our stressors. I will continue to take one day at a time. I will continue to take my medications, see my doctor routinely, and surround myself with the love and support of my family. I believe I have found me. I have found the love of my life, I love my work, and I love myself. I figured out why I am here on earth and will continue to grow personally, and I have conquered my fear of death.

I know and believe in the afterlife. I have personally experienced it when my dad was dying. When I was in the hospital, I had to make the decision to live my life or to pass over into the afterlife. I have had many friends share their experiences with loved ones that have passed over and near misses of their own.

I believe our spirit, our physical form, comes to earth and helps loved ones through life while here on earth. I believe in all the signs from heaven from our loved ones. I see and experience them almost daily. My vivid dream was just more validation for me of the afterlife to come and the fact that we are all here on earth for a reason. I believe God has our plan set before we even get here, and it plays out for us just like he has planned—whether we are here for a short time and we die as a baby; whether we live to be a teenager and die an unexpected death; or whether we live to be a wise old lady or man and share our stories with those we love. We learn from all of our life experiences, and we teach others from our own experiences. What happens to us throughout our childhood and our entire lives determines our strengths and weaknesses. It makes us the human beings that we are— whether we are kind and compassionate or hard-hearted, or if we become unkind and evil. We make our own destiny by what we choose to do with the experiences we have had. It is totally up to us.

Even though I came from a sexually, mentally, and physically abusive childhood, I still chose to be compassionate and loving, and I give my all to everything I do. The experiences in my life have been hard, but I have chosen to be the best person I can be and to stop the cycle of abuse. I wish I had been stronger through the years that my children were growing up so I could have saved them from the emotional abuse that I feel they endured because of my dealing with my childhood and my undiagnosed bipolar I and PTSD. I hope someday my children will learn that this is what has helped form them into the strong, loving adults that they are today.

For you, the readers, I hope the story of my journey has shown you how strong we as human beings are. I hope that you can look back on your past, your childhood, and see the good times that you had. Realize that every one of us has a story to tell, a journey that we have traveled. Not all stories are sugarcoated, but we need to see the good in them. We need to make the best of what God has set before us and to make the choice to change our own behaviors; in doing so we can change not just how we feel about ourselves—we can change the life of someone we love. Make the choice to be the best person you can be. Peace and light to you and your family, and I will see you in the afterlife.

Finding Me

Through all the abuse, through all the pain I walk,
I searched through the crowd to find me.
It seems like a lifetime.
I did not know how or when, but I knew I would,
I would find me.
I walk through life with my head held high.
I can look back and see how far I have come.
It has been a journey, a struggle, I know.
Without all I have seen, I wouldn't have been able to see.
I would not have been able to love, to grow, to be.
Without all that I have seen and felt, I would not have been able to
Find me.

CHAPTER 22

Not Yet

Is it a curse, or is it a gift? I thought I was done, done with my journey. I hear it, and I feel it. *"Not yet."*

In writing my book I have been guided. Is it by God or by the Angels? I believe it is both. When I hear that little voice or have what is called a "knowing" I must pay attention to it.

I have one more thing to share. I'm not clear as to the why of it sometimes; I just know I am guided to do it. To say it, to share it. There are those of you who share this gift, and you will understand. Those of you who don't have it can get hope or inspiration. It may even renew a faith you have lost.

I have been drawn to share with you a journal entry. I journal frantically as I experience my manic episodes. This is an entry from my June 2014 stay at the mental facility that I have stayed at three times.

The Visit

As I walk the halls, reality hits me in the face. A friend of mine is a patient here. I sit and talk with her. God yet again throws myself at me. She shares with me just a glimpse of her story. Just enough to help me realize why God has sent me here.

I am here for a purpose, and that is to spread the word. My journey has been deep, and no one knows just how heavy it has been. No one but Him.

I fear if I sleep, I will lose my gift, my creativity, my color, my art, my love, and my life. I need to write. I don't want to forget. I want to remember, to put it all down.

I question myself. How far after I wake, will I be able to walk? Will I stay the course and finish what He sent me here to do? I fear in reality that God only wants me to live a simple life. My heart wants to do good. Good for all. I want to spread the love, the faith, the hope, and the life.

If I can fix myself with help, it will help others to follow.

My work will be done if I only find my own path.

Let the rest go. Sleep, baby, sleep.

Daddy

It's been a year today since my first words were put to paper.

My journey through abuse has come to an end.

As I sit and write, I realize I am listening to Patsy again. She helps me feel closer to you somehow. As Father's Day approaches, I think I should feel sad. I don't. Yes, I miss you; yes, I love you. I know we will be together again someday.

Daddy, I thank you for doing the best that you could.

Daddy, I love you for the good times.

I thank you for changing when you did.

Daddy, I thank you for being you.

All my love, your little girl, Bella.

ABOUT THE AUTHOR

Bella Louise Allen has had a love for writing since high school. This is just the beginning of her journey with writing. Her first book shares with you her journey, not just with her love for writing but also the struggles she has encountered over the years and how important writing has been in her own therapy along the way.

When Bella is not creating magic on paper, you can find her taking care of those she loves and working hard to provide for her family and herself. She also loves to travel to beautiful parts of her state (Maine) and capture the beauty of the state and memories with her family.

Please visit this website to know more about the author:

foxbangor.com-bangor.mainewviiabc7
julieyoung57@yahoo.com

Printed in the United States
By Bookmasters